T0072301

OTIS'
ODYSSEY

HOW TO FLY AND STAY ALIVE

OTIS

authorHOUSE

AuthorHouse™
1663 Liberty Drive
Bloomington, IN 47403
www.authorhouse.com
Phone: 833-262-8899

Published by AuthorHouse 02/14/2023

ISBN: 979-8-8230-0106-9 (sc)
ISBN: 979-8-8230-0107-6 (e)

Library of Congress Control Number: 2023903008

Print information available on the last page.

CONTENTS

CHAPTER 1

OTIS'S ODYSSEY

I was born on May 3, 1941, at St. Mary's Hospital in San Francisco, California; went to a Catholic school; and became an altar boy at our local church. I then transferred to Luther Burbank Junior High School in Visitation Valley but hung around a rowdy crowd and eventually belonged to a local gang. We were kind of harmless, being more talk than action, and the most dangerous weapon we carried was a pair of brass knuckles. Smoking cigarettes was cool, as was wearing matching jackets and suede shoes while walking down the streets of San Francisco and watching the other gangs.

Saturday night dances in the basement of someone's house with the lights turned down low and a forty-five-revolutions-per-minute record playing "Earth Angel" by the Penguins was the closest we could get to the opposite sex.

When I was fourteen years old, I delivered the *Chronicle* newspaper in the morning on my bicycle, and every time I would ride by this one house, I noticed a 1955 Buick four-door hardtop parked outside with all the windows down and the keys in the ignition. One morning, Steve Lavezzo, who had another paper route, and I got into the car but couldn't start it. We eventually discovered that the starter button for that model was located underneath the gas pedal that would automatically put fuel into the carburetor as the engine would turn over. We would drive around while delivering our papers, go out to Play Land at the beach for a joyride, and then return the car to the house before anyone woke up. This lasted for a week or so until we stopped. We later found out the owner would come home drunk every night and forget to lock his car. I bet he thought he was getting lousy gas mileage for those couple of weeks.

After a few years, I managed to save up $300 that I used to buy my first car, a 1951 Mercury four-door sedan with getaway doors (rear doors that opened forward). I was only fifteen and a half years old and had a permit that allowed me to drive with an adult, but that didn't stop me. One day, I got caught by myself and told the police I was just going to the store to pick up a loaf of bread for my mother. The police didn't buy it, and I was grounded until I got my license.

Well, I was the most popular kid in my neighborhood when I finally started driving, and every morning, I would pick up all my classmates for Balboa High School. One morning when I pulled up in front of school, eleven people got out of my car. And of course, I never had to buy any gas. On Friday nights, we would go to the drive-in theater, and I was the only one in the car. But after I parked, I would open the trunk, and three of my friends would get out. That Mercury was also a great place for heavy petting with some of my girlfriends, but that's about as far as I would get.

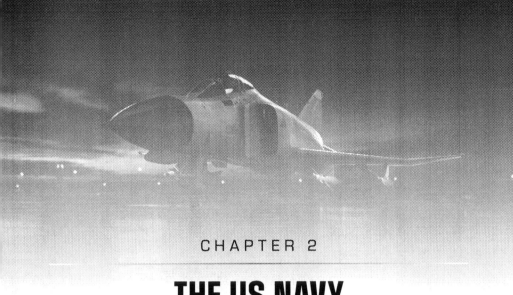

CHAPTER 2

THE US NAVY

High school was not my best achievement. In fact, I barely graduated because I was busy chasing girls and getting into trouble. I attended San Francisco Community College for a couple of years but still couldn't keep my mind on my studies and eventually transferred to Cogswell Poly Technical College, where I received an associate's degree in electronics. Because of the Vietnam War and the draft, I tried to enlist in the aviation cadet program at Alameda Naval Air Station but was told Cogswell was not an accredited college. So, my drafting instructor, a retired rear admiral, went to Alameda with all the legal documents. And on October 12, 1963, I was accepted.

I was sent to Pensacola, Florida, as a cadet for a sixteen-week preflight program that consisted of academic, physical, and military training, sort of a crash course of the naval academy. On November 22, 1963, I was being fitted for my uniform when I heard on the radio that President John F. Kennedy had been assassinated. I'll remember that day for the rest of my life.

One weekend, a few classmates and I went swimming off a pier. I dove into shallow water and hit my head, fracturing my jaw. That took two weeks to heal and sent me back to the next flight class. After graduation, we were sent to whatever training we or the navy desired, such as fighter, bomber, submarine patrol, or helicopter aircraft. It seemed like all the smart guys with bachelor's degrees would wind up flying slower aircraft, while us dumb guys were assigned to fighters. The navy wanted fighter pilots to react to a situation and not spend too much time thinking about it, or they might get shot down.

After twelve months of advanced training, I received my commission as an ensign, along with my navy wings. Then I was sent to VF121 for two months at Miramar Naval Air Station near San Diego, California, flying in the F-4B Phantom II. We had a pilot in the training squadron who crashed three F-4s before the navy finally decided to take his wings away and assign him a ground billet. Well, after he was discharged, he went to medical school and became a surgeon. I guess he was too smart to fly.

In January 1964, I was assigned to the VF-161 Chargers at Miramar, flying in the Phantom. Because of my electronics background, I was in charge of the weapons department in the squadron. One night, my men invited me to Poway, a town north of Miramar, for a cookout. Well, I had too many beers; on the way home in my 1962 Pontiac Tempest Convertible, I lost control on a winding road and rolled the car over. As I was rolling, I managed to fasten my seat belt, and when the Tempest came to rest, I was hanging from the strap. I crawled out and walked back to a gas station I'd passed to call my roommate. When I returned to the scene of the accident, the police were hiking down an embankment looking for the driver. I tried to act as sober as I could. When I told the police officers I was the driver and that I flew fighters out of Miramar, they put me in the back of their squad car and drove me to the BOQ and said, "Good luck fighting the war in Vietnam." The police were very tolerant in those days because of the war.

The senior officers in the squadron would invite the junior officers to the officers' club and get us drunk and then take advantage of us the next day in dogfights because we would black out sooner pulling g's and lose sight of the other planes.

We had a squadron commander who would always have a couple of martinis before dinner and then fly a night intercept flight. After he retired, he went to work flying charter flights from San Francisco to Reno. One night, he crashed into a mountain, killing everyone on board. If they could have done an autopsy, I'd bet there was alcohol in his blood.

Our squadron went to Yuma Marine Corps Air Station in Arizona for two weeks to practice our bombing techniques against the marines. Every evening after flying, we would go to the officers' club for a few drinks and square off with those grunts. One night, we bet the marines they couldn't drink flaming hookers, which consisted of lighting brandy in a shot glass and drinking it without burning your face; only we had their drinks put into champagne glasses. I guess those marines weren't too bright because they would try to toss that brandy down, and their entire face and hair would catch on fire. The next day, their faces were so blistered they couldn't even put on their oxygen masks when they went flying. I guess that's why they're called jarheads.

One weekend, some of us drove to San Luis, south of the border, to see some girls we'd met a few days before. Well, my date couldn't make it. So she sent her fourteen-year-old sister, who allowed me to take her virginity. Only in Mexico!

The Phantom is a twin-engine, two-seat fighter producing 34,000 pounds of thrust and weighing 58,000 pounds. Max Allison and I always flew together so we could anticipate what the other person was going to do. Part of our training was high-altitude interception while wearing a pressure suit that was filled with oxygen in case of depressurization. We made a run on a drone coming out of Point Mugu NAS in Oxnard, California, at 78,000 feet and had to make a profile approach by climbing to 40,000 feet, pushing the nose over to gain Mach airspeed, and then pulling the nose above the horizon to acquire the target.

We launched a Sparrow II Missile at 62,000 feet at Mach 2.1 (1,330 miles per hour). As the missile left the aircraft, the exhaust disrupted the airflow to our intakes and flamed out booth engines. We immediately lost pressurization, and our suits became stiff with oxygen, making it difficult to fly the aircraft. For what seemed like an eternity, we were just a projectile in the thin atmosphere—until the nose gradually dropped below the horizon, allowing us to gain airspeed. The engines finally started to windmill, giving us enough revolutions per minute for an air start, but we had lost 14,000 feet before complete control of the aircraft was obtained. The air controller said we had hit our target, making us the first ones to intercept a drone at that altitude. While we were at 62,000 feet, we could see the curvature of the earth, and the sky was so dark in the middle of the day that stars appeared.

One day a friend of mine, Robert Anton, was returning to Miramar from a reconnaissance training mission in an F-8 Crusader. As he turned on final approach, he experienced a complete hydraulic failure and decided to turn the aircraft away from the populated field to eject. Wouldn't you know it that the Crusader banked back toward the field after he ejected and crashed into a hangar, killing several people? Then while Max was parachuting down, he landed in a parking lot and got hit by a car.

A couple weeks later, our squadron accepted an air force exchange pilot who thought he was the best F-4 jock in the country. But after being sent out to sea for carrier qualifications, he became very humble when he had trouble getting that Phantom on the deck. We went to NAS Fallon, Nevada, for some more bombing practice but this air force captain was always trying unusual maneuvers with the aircraft. One day after returning from a bombing mission with three other F-4s in an echelon formation, he decided to try a tuck under break over the field. When he pulled up and rolled over, he came down on the aircraft next to him canopy to canopy, killing himself and ejecting his partner, who was found later in a field alive with all his limbs broken. I guess if he hadn't killed himself here in the United States, he would have done it in Vietnam.

A few days after the accident, four of us went out in the desert to shoot some rabbits and get away from that squadron for a while. Max Allison took his 1963 Corvette Stingray coupe with a 427cu engine, and I took my 1964 Corvette convertible with a 327cu engine. We decided to find out how fast those cars would go. I had gotten mine up to 145 miles per hour when, all of a sudden, Max passed me like I was standing still—must have been those solid lifters his engine had.

CHAPTER 3

VIETNAM

The fun was over, and it was time to go to war. We deployed in May 1966 from San Diego on the USS *Constellation* (CV-64). It had just been overhauled in Bremerton, Washington' with the latest electronics; had a crew of five thousand and a deck that was the length of two football fields; and weighed eighty thousand tons. The air wing consisted of two F-4B Phantom fighter squadrons, two A-4C Skyhawk attack squadrons, one RA-5C vigilante reconnaissance attack squadron, one A-6A intruder attack squadron, one A-3B Skywarrior heavy attack refueling squadron, and one E-2A Hawkeye airborne early warning squadron—totaling some eighty aircraft. Our first stop was Pearl Harbor, Hawaii, for an operational readiness inspection and some R & R. Then we were on to Yokuska, Japan, for flagship duties. Next, we went to Subic Bay, Philippines, for supplies. And finally, we arrived at Yankee Station in the Gulf of Tonkin to start our first combat missions against North Vietnam. Because we'd purposely bombed poorly during our training deployments in the United States, our sister F-4 squadron was assigned to most of the more dangerous missions of close air support dropping bombs, while we were assigned the "MiG" patrols.

On Friday, July 13, 1966, three strike groups consisting of over fifty aircraft went to Hanoi to bomb airfields and oil storages in the

Haiphong Harbor. The strike included the air force in the morning, a navy air strike two hours later, and then another air force strike in the afternoon. The sky was full of MiGs, both from North Vietnam and Communist China. You could tell the difference because the North Vietnamese pilots would hit and run, while the more experienced Chinese pilots would stay and fight.

Max and I came across a couple of late-model MiG 17 Frescos with afterburners and nose radar that were firing their rockets at our A-4 Skyhawks, which were making a bombing run on the Co Trai Bridge. We launched an AIM-7E Sparrow missile at one of the MiGs that detonated on a cloud, but at least they broke off their attack and split up. We hit our afterburner, pulled up, and passed canopy to canopy with one MiG, and when I looked up, I saw a gray helmet with a red star on it, which made me believe he was a Communist Chinese pilot.

We were at eight thousand feet when he decided to dive for the deck. We did a slow rudder reversal, which got us on his tail and then chased him down to treetop level, locked him up on radar at about two miles, got a growl in our headsets, and launched an AIM-9D Sidewinder missile that went right up his tailpipe. We pulled up and looked for a parachute before the MiG hit the ground but didn't see anything.

You're trained to win the fight over the other aircraft but kind of hope the other pilot makes it out alive. The fight that took about two minutes seemed like two hours, and I'd never had so much adrenalin running through my body in my life.

Realizing we were low on fuel, we headed for the coastline and managed to find an A-3 "Texaco in the Sky" and, after a nervous approach, plugged in and got a tank of gas.

When we arrived at the carrier, we asked to do a victory roll, which told everyone on board what had transpired. Well, Max—whose last name was changed to "MiG" Guigan—and I received the Distinguished Flying Cross (DFC) for downing that MiG, and Friday the thirteenth has been my lucky day ever since.

After spending thirty-five days on station and countless sorties, it was time for a little rest and relaxation. The *Constellation* headed for Hong Kong but wasn't allowed in the harbor because of the ordnance we were carrying, so sampans would come out and take us to the mainland. Hong Kong, owned by the British at the time, was the most beautiful place I'd ever seen. You could eat at restaurants with food from all over the world, have custom-made clothes and shoes made for a tenth of what it would cost in the United States, and be treated like a king at any hotel.

The commanding officer of our squadron gave a party in a ballroom on the fortieth floor of the Hong Kong Hilton in Kowloon across the bay from Hong Kong. Most of the pilots' wives had flown in from the United States, and the rest of us bachelors brought local dates. We had a magnificent dinner and then some of the squadron members would perform skits on stage about happenings during our time on station. When the party was over, it was time for the old cronies and their wives to find a quiet lounge, while us young bucks headed for the discos. We filed out of the ballroom toward the elevators, but the first two were immediately filled up, leaving my date and me to wait. She was a pretty, petite nineteen-year-old Chinese/Portuguese model who spoke fairly good English, and I'd met her a couple days earlier.

Well, the third elevator finally arrived, and when we got in, we saw it was plush with wall-to-wall carpet and mirrors on the ceiling. As we descended, we looked at one another and thought, *What the hell?* So, I managed to wedge my shoe in the door, and the elevator stopped between the fifteenth and sixteenth floors, and when the alarm didn't sound, we took off our clothes and made love on that plush carpet.

We lost track of time, and after removing my shoe from the door, we started back down to the lobby. When the door opened, the entire squadron was lined up on either side as far as you could see applauding. I guess they noticed the elevator stopped between floors and figured out what we were up to.

The commanding officer approached me; looked down at the name on the elevator; shook my hand; and said, "Congratulations, 'Otis.'" Well the skipper has the authorization at sea and officially changed my name to Otis for the rest of the tour.

We were back on station, but now I was flying with David Day because Max had been rotated back to the States to become an instructor pilot at Key West, Florida. On his way to Florida with his new wife, he got into an accident in his Pontiac GTO and then had a midair collision with a student pilot during a night intercept mission, but he's still alive thank god. Fessler was more senior than me and was married with seven children, including two sets of twins. He was a little nervous and drank a lot. In fact, one morning, he locked himself in his cabin so he didn't have to fly because he'd been drinking all night. A lot of that went on, and the skipper would usually work things out.

One day, a pilot walked into the commanding officer's cabin and placed his gold wings on his desk and said his wife didn't want him to fly anymore. All the skipper could do was assign him to a ground billet.

Bob and I flew through the month of August with only a couple of close calls. On one flight while rolling in on a pontoon bridge at Thanh Hóa, the small arms fire was so intense it looked like golf balls and Roman candles streaking by our canopy. On another flight, while escorting an RA-3 reconnaissance plane, we got hit aft of our auxiliary air doors by 37–57mm because that A-3 was flying too damn slow.

One day, David Day, who was the maintenance officer, let France Davison, another pilot, and I take an F-4 to Cubi Point in the Philippines for some maintenance. While the crew there were working on the plane, John and I caught a hop on a military transport to Bangkok, Thailand, where my aunt was living because my uncle was an engineer working in South Vietnam. She put us up for a few days, and since John and I both played tennis, she arranged a doubles match on the lawn at the sports arena with the premiere of Bangkok. It was a very memorable time because the premiere acted like any other individual with a great sense of humor.

The carrier came into Subic Bay for more replenishments and much needed R & R, with everyone usually adjourning to the Cubi O club. One night, we set up a replica of a carrier arrestment, where a person would lie down on the bar, and the rest of us would catapult him toward the dining area. Well, one guy didn't get his foot down in time to stop and shot off the bar and landed on the admiral's table, spilling food and wine everywhere. The admiral got up, shook the guy's hand, and said he should practice those carrier landings a little more. If that happened any place else there would have been a court martial, but it was in time of war, and nobody took things too seriously.

One other night, the club brought in some live entertainment, and while the gals were on stage singing, one guy crawled up into the ceiling. When he got over the stage, the roof gave way, and he crashed down on top of those girls. Well, it didn't take long for the manager to see that things were getting out of control, and he hustled those girls out of there and onto a helicopter in record time.

There was a town nearby called Olongapo, where Philippine kids would dive in sewage water under a bridge for coins tossed by sailors.

I went into a lounge one night and sat at the bar and ordered a San Miguel beer. A guy on the bar stool next to me had a girl sitting on his lap; it took me awhile to realize they were having sex without anybody else in the place knowing. On Christmas Eve, I met a good Catholic Philippine girl who took me to church to pray with her and then took me home and gave me a case of gonorrhea.

It was the end of 1966, and the cruise was finally over. I'd flown ninety-nine combat missions, and it was time to go home. While we were transferring fuel from a tanker one day on our way back to San Diego, the sea was so rough the *Constellation* was taking water over the flight deck, which was sixty feet from the surface. The tanker almost disappeared in the ocean, with several men washing overboard, keeping our helicopter very busy picking them up. And can you believe they still transferred the fuel?

When we were about five hundred miles from San Diego, they launched the aircraft so they could fly over the families waiting at Miramar Naval Station. The weather was overcast with a ceiling at two hundred feet that extended up to three thousand feet. As Bob and I launched and started climbing through the solid overcast, we were waiting to break out and see the sunny sky, but instead, we saw water. The horizontal situation indicator was lagging, and the aircraft had rolled inverted, while the instruments showed we were still in a climb. We immediately rolled the wings level, pulled back on the stick, and saw the altimeter go below zero. I don't know what kept that Phantom from hitting the water, but it sure scared the hell out of both of us.

My time in San Diego was not the same. Everyone acted very recklessly, both flying and in general, because of the war we had seen. One weekend, a friend of mine, who was a Navy SEAL got married and had his wedding on a three-deck party boat in Mission Bay. After a couple of hours, they ran out of liquor. So, some of us took off our tuxedos with our swim trunks underneath and swam a mile to shore to the nearest bar.

I lived in a large house on the top of Mount Soledad with three other aviators, and one night while driving up the winding road in my Corvette, I hit a tree in a front yard and trapped my girlfriend's head between the steering wheel and my crotch. Well, you should have seen the look on the faces of the people who came to help us out of the car.

Hell, it was August 1967, and we were already going back to Vietnam but this time on the USS *Coral Sea* (CV-43), a smaller retrofitted World War II carrier. It was a little harder to get aboard because there were only four arresting cables, instead of the five that were on the *Constellation*. We also had the last propeller squadron, the A-1 Skyraider, that the deck crew wasn't used to because you didn't see that prop turning.

One day, a plane captain was backing up while guiding an F-4 and walked right into a prop that nearly cut him in half; at least when a guy is sucked down a jet intake he's protected by a screen.

We'd been on station for about a month, and the deck was getting slippery from the jet fuel and oil. And when an aircraft isn't launching or taxiing, it's chained down. An F-4 got the nose wheel stuck on the arresting cable, and when he powered up to break free, his exhaust blew an A-4 that was unchained right over the side and into the water. The pilot, who was the commanding officer of his squadron, ejected inverted but was killed by the impact with the water.

The war had escalated since last year. with more traffic on the roads from North Vietnam to South Vietnam, more antiaircraft fire. and more SAM sites. And now the Russians were involved, supplying the Communists with everything. On one strike flight near Hanoi, our sister squadron lost three F-4s to Chinese pilots coming down from the border; it didn't seem like the war was fair. Two days later, there were six new replacement crewmen in their ready room who nobody knew; it was hard to keep your sanity sometimes.

Bob and I were on patrol one day when the whole sky lit up with SAMs. Our wingman got hit and went down in flames, and I saw a SAM explode off our wing and thought we were dead; the plane rocked and rolled but managed to remain undamaged, and I pissed my pants.

The weather this year was extremely poor. Not only did you get shot at, but sometimes it was difficult to find the carrier and land on a pitching deck. During a night carrier landing, our executive officer touched down long, missing all the arresting cables and then they to take off (bolter), but his nose dropped over the bow. Afterburner and back stick didn't stop the nose of that heavy Phantom, and they plunged into the water, at which time the carrier ran over the plane, killing both crewmen.

One F-4 landed on the wrong carrier one day, and before they were catapulted off again the flight deck crew had painted their logos on the plane. what an embarrassment when they got back to the *Coral Sea*.

Only the F-4s were on condition watch twenty-four hours around the clock, and one night while Bob and I were sitting in our cockpits, two ground crewmen were racing their equipment on the flight deck. They backed up to the fantail, raced their engines, and then put them into gear to accelerate down the flight deck. But one guy put his in reverse and backed over the side. They launched the search-and-rescue helicopter and recovered him, but the sailor lost six months of his pay for that stunt.

On return from a hop, Bob and I were diverted to Da Nang, South Vietnam, because of a hung bomb. Since we had a low fuel state, we climbed to twenty-five thousand feet to conserve fuel en route and then let down through the clouds, hoping to find the coastline. We broke out at eight hundred feet and then followed the coast south to Da Nang. But by the time we found the runway, we were flying on fumes. After touchdown, one of the engines flamed out on the runway, and the other one flamed out just as we parked the aircraft. No wonder my hair had become prematurely gray.

We spent the night in a hotel, but I never slept because of the continuous mortar shelling around town. But the local boys said you'd get used to it. The next day, we couldn't fly out of there quickly enough. And would you believe the Vietcong hiding outside the base started shooting at us on takeoff?

Once in a while, we would have a stand-down day, and the flight deck would fill with sailors enjoying barbecues, pie-eating contests, boxing, judo, weight-lifting matches, touch football, and of course entertainment. Bob Hope brought his USO entourage, including Raquel Welch, Elaine Dunn, Barbara McNair, Madeleine Hartog (Miss World from Peru), and some dancers; and you'd never believe there was a war going on. God bless that bunch. Not only did they visit the ships, they also went in country, which wasn't very safe at times. "Thanks for the memories, Bob."

A couple of days later the carrier USS *Saratoga* started smoking on the horizon. Apparently while an ordnance man was loading flares on the hangar deck, he dropped one, and instead of pushing it over the side, he ran. When the flare ignited, it set the rest into a blaze nobody could put out. The next day when the fire was finally extinguished, it had melted half the bow of the ship, killing hundreds of people, including the officers who died in their sleep. As ironic as it was, the kid who dropped the flare lived.

It was February 17, 1968, and the war was over for me at least. I'd flown 210 combat missions, more than anyone on the ship; received a DFC, sixteen Air Medals, three Navy Commendation Medals, a Navy Unit Commendation Medal, a Navy Defense Service Medal, an Armed Forces Reserve Medal, two Vietnam Service Medals, a Vietnam Gallantry Cross, and a Vietnam Commendation Medal. I would say the Navy got its money's worth out of me; now it was time to go home.

While the *Coral Sea* was in Subic Bay for replenishment and R & R, I stayed on the ship as the duty officer and had a yeoman friend of mine write my separation orders, including two weeks in Hong Kong as a liaison officer, and nobody was the wiser. The *Coral Sea* left Subic Bay without me to the Sea of Japan to cover the USS *Pueblo* incident, where Captain Bucher and his crew were captured by the North Koreans for spying.

While relaxing in Hong Kong, my Chinese model friend said she wanted to get married and come back to the United States with me. Well, I wasn't ready to settle down yet, so I flew back to Treasure Island Naval Station across the bay from San Francisco for discharge. And would you believe the Navy paid me for those two weeks of liaison in Hong Kong?

While I was in Hong Kong, I'd met a navy lieutenant who was transferring to Virginia, so we traveled together. After my discharge, we loaded up my Corvette and headed to Tulsa, Oklahoma, to see an American girl I'd met in Japan. When I found her, she was engaged to be married. So I said the hell with this and took the lieutenant to the airport and then headed back to Aspen, Colorado, to do a little snow skiing.

On my first day down the hill, I hit a mogul and broke my ankle and spent the next two months in a cast helping the owners of a hotel I was staying at run it. An amputee demonstration team was staying at the hotel, and I met an army captain who'd lost his leg from a mine in Vietnam. He hadn't gotten his prosthesis yet, so we would go out at night to the bars on our crutches, falling down drunk in the snow. He would sit at the bar and wait for a girl to sit next to him, and after some conversation, he would put her hand on his knee until it slipped off at the stub; if it didn't bother her, he'd take her home.

One beautiful amputee girl at the hotel had lost her leg in an automobile accident. After a couple of drinks, she spent the night with me. While I was waiting in bed for her with the lights out, she took off her prosthesis and hopped across the room—hard to concentrate sometimes.

One other night, I was with a girl who'd broken the opposite leg (from the one I'd broken), and while we were making love, I broke her damn cast.

CHAPTER 4

CIVILIAN LIFE

I finally went back to South Mission Beach in San Diego for a couple of years, going to school, working construction, smoking marijuana, taking LSD, and trying to figure out what to do with my life. I joined the naval reserves and was a weekend warrior at Los Alamitos Naval Air Station near Long Beach, flying in the F-4B Phantom. The extra money was great, but we were vulnerable to being recalled to active duty at any time.

On March 6, 1970, I managed to be the first reservist to graduate from the Top Gun Fighter Weapons Course at NAS Miramar. I started flying civilian aircraft at Montgomery Field in San Diego, getting my commercial and flight instructor licenses with instrument and multi-engine ratings but ran out of money and reached my first low.

Then I met a United Airlines stewardess and followed her to Fresno, California, to meet her father, who owned nine thousand acres on the west side. He said, if I married his daughter, I would never have to worry about money again. But she was too bossy, and it wasn't worth the trouble.

I went to work for Denair Aviation, a Cessna Dealership at Chandler Field near Fresno, teaching flying; chartering; and, eventually, selling aircraft. Most of my customers were farmers with their own airstrips, and if you could make that Cessna perform better than the competitors, they would buy it.

Fresno was a party town and the farm girls were very healthy and sexually active. I belonged to a reserve unit at Point Mugu NAS near Oxnard, California, and would fly a Cessna down once a month for the meetings. During a two-week active duty period, I was assigned to an EC-121K Constellation Aircraft tracking a guided missile from Vandenberg AFB four thousand miles downrange to Kwajalein located in the Marshall Islands. On our way back in Hawaii I got drunk, fell down, and broke my jaw for the second time.

While selling airplanes I was always trying to fly that Cessna to the limit, and one day, I took a Turbo 210 Centurion to Escalon near Sacramento to show a farmer who had his own airstrip. His old plane was an STOL (short-field takeoff and landing) T-210 because of his short strip. Well I landed OK. After writing up an order for a new Centurion with an STOL, I departed but realized his runway was too short for my T-210. As I rotated, I struck a standpipe and ripped open the belly of the plane, barely missing the elevator cables in the tail. I flew back to Chandler Field that night and put the plane in the maintenance hangar and had the skin removed so the Federal Aviation Administration (FAA) wouldn't find out. One day, an inspector from the FAA came by, and the maintenance department told him the plane had been damaged in the hangar.

I sold a pressurized Cessna 414 in San Ardo south of Salinas to Gordon Rosenberg, who also had his own airstrip, where he kept a Breezy, an open cockpit, two-seat, high-wing tandem aircraft. One weekend, I took it up with a girlfriend of mine, and while we were flying down the Salinas River, I struck a power cable that almost decapitated us when it snapped. After landing, Gordon, who was a volunteer firefighter, was heading to a brushfire on the Salinas River that I later found out was caused by the power cable I'd severed.

During a demonstration flight in a Cessna 340 coming back from Mexico with five Mexican cowboys, I did an aileron roll while they were sleeping with all the window curtains closed. They knew something had happened, but every time they tried to stand up, their equilibrium was amiss, and they kept falling down. What a sight.

After showing a new C-177 Cardinal in Merced, I was flying south along Highway 99 to Fresno when the engine quit. So, I glided down and landed on a frontage road. The fuel gage showed half a tank. But when I looked in the wings, they were bone dry; never trust your gages. A farmer let me use his phone to call Denair Aviation to get some fuel brought up, but while I was waiting, a highway patrol drove by and decided to exit the freeway and come back. So, I asked the farmer if he would act like I was showing him the airplane. After the patrolman left, the fuel arrived, and there we were alongside the freeway pumping gas into the plane, hoping not to get caught. As soon as we got enough gas to get me to Fresno I got the hell out of there—another lucky day.

One other time, I landed on a farmer's grass strip with a Mooney. But he had just irrigated the area, and the grass was so slick I couldn't stop with his house and a gas pump directly in front of me. I locked the left rudder and brake, spun the plane around, and collapsed the right landing gear just a few feet from that gas pump. Well that Mooney sat there for a couple of months while our maintenance department was waiting for parts. And when the FAA heard about it, the farmer said he was taxiing and hit a ditch; it's nice to have farmer friends.

After seven years and seven accidents demonstrating those airplanes; selling more T-210s than anyone in the nation one year; and taking girls up to join the one-, two-, and three-mile high clubs, I asked the company if I could be a part owner. When they said no, I moved to Chico, north of Sacramento, and went into partnership with another Cessna operator. I busted my ass for a year, only to find out that my partner had embezzled over $100,000 of our profit and taken off for South America.

I didn't want anything to do with airplanes after that, so I went to work on an almond farm in Durham for a year, driving heavy equipment and enjoying myself more than I had in a long time. I was transferred to a navy reserve unit in Sacramento and was assigned a project that took me to the Aleutian Islands. A navy reserve chief petty officer and I spent two weeks documenting conditions of airfields on

Adak, Kamchitka, Kiska, Shimya, and Attu, bringing back over 750 photographs. That two-week cruise along with a 4.0 fitness report from an admiral at Adak Naval Air Station promoted me to commander in the naval reserves.

One day, while I was leveling 350 acres with a D-8 tractor in Durham, I was informed by the owner that my sister had called from Santa Rosa to say my father had died of prostate cancer. Well after that news, a failed aircraft business, and not much money, I reached another low in my life.

CHAPTER 5

THE ACCIDENT

I quit the farming business after a year and went to work for Vindar Aviation, a Cessna dealership at Gnoss Field in Novato, north of San Francisco. I owned a C-172 Skyhawk that I would fly back to Durham on the weekends, where I lived in a house on an almond orchard with a nineteen-year-old local girl. For once, life seemed to be treating me well again.

Vindar had a flight school, a maintenance department, and a charter service and sold new and used aircraft, including Beechcraft and Pipers. On Sunday, September 27, 1982, Daryl Scott, the manager/owner of Vindar, telephoned me in Durham, giving my girlfriend a false name so I would come to the phone. He said he had a customer in Longmont, Colorado, who wanted to buy the 1971 Piper Aztec we had for sale. The condition of the sale was that the plane had to be delivered by midnight that night, or the sale would be terminated. I asked him why he couldn't get a pilot from the flight department to ferry the aircraft, and he said nobody was checked out in the plane and that only I could close the sale, with a guaranteed $1,500 commission.

The Aztec, which had over five thousand hours of flying time on the airframe, came from Alaska, where it had been used for charter service; had had several gear-up landing accidents and questionable maintenance records; and was instrument equipped but hadn't been certified for the past ten years. Vindar did the annual inspection on the aircraft in half the time it normally takes to save money, leaving doubts as to what exactly was inspected.

I flew my Skyhawk from Chico to Sonoma County Airport, where I had left my Ranchero, and then drove down to Gnoss Field, arriving about two o'clock that afternoon, later than I had anticipated. With an extensive preflight inspection on the Aztec, I decided to take the flight. I had trouble starting the engines because the batteries were low and had to get a jump from the mechanic, getting me into the air at four o'clock, four hours later than I had planned. Gnoss Field is an uncontrolled airfield with no tower, so I couldn't check out the radios properly. There was a storm along my route, but it was clear in Colorado. So, I climbed to 11,500 feet and headed for Sacramento.

The first thing I noticed was the autopilot was inoperative, and the heater didn't work. But I continued the flight that would take me to Tonopah, Nevada; Cedar City, Utah; and then Longmont near Denver, Colorado, with a flying time of about four hours. I attempted to contact Oakland Center for flight following but was unable to channel the frequencies on either radio. Only one VOR navigation instrument was working, but since I was VFR (visual flying rules), I proceeded with the flight.

As I passed over Tonopah, it was starting to get dark and cold. So, I put on an extra pair of clothes, including socks on my hands. There was a cold front coming down from Alaska and a warm current from a hurricane coming up from Baja California ahead of me. But it was clear in Denver. I thought about landing at Tonopah, but I'd flown through many storms before, and since it was clear on the other side, I didn't think there would be a problem.

As I entered the clouds and started flying by instruments, I discovered the horizontal situation indicator, which gives attitude information, was unreliable. Because the Aztec had dual controls and dual instruments, I took off my safety harness and moved to the right seat to fly. I was homing in on Cedar City when I noticed the wings starting to accumulate some rime ice, but I was holding altitude at

11,000 feet. And then it happened—a bright flash across the windshield and then a jolt through the aircraft, causing my hair to stand on end. I had been hit by a bolt of lightning and could see arcs of electricity running across the dashboard out to the wings and discharging off the trailing edges.

As the lightning kept striking the aircraft, the instrument panel lights got dimmer; apparently I had lost both alternators and regulators. I tried to recycle the alternators, but there wasn't enough power in the batteries to excite the system. I took out my flashlight that had fairly new batteries, but it only lasted about three minutes. I even used up a book of matches trying to see the instrument panel. Without any lights, I had trouble keeping the wings level. And when the lightning would flash, I would have a few seconds to look at the instrument panel and control the aircraft.

Airplanes have always been built to fly straight and level by themselves, so I took my hands off the controls and lowered the landing gear and flaps, and with a little trim, the aircraft eventually leveled itself.

My next problem was to descend below the cloud layer and get rid of the ice on the wings. I had estimated myself to be over a valley near the town of Caliente north of Las Vegas. I reduced the power and descended at about 300 feet per minute, both by feel and by noticing the rate of descent indicator when the lightning would flash. At about 7,000 feet, the ice on the wings started melting, and the plane became more controllable. At about 3,000 feet above the ground, I broke out below the overcast and saw the lights of a town I believed to be Caliente.

I flew the aircraft by using the limited horizon of the town and the overcast and eventually saw a highway I believed to be 93, which went south to Las Vegas. Unfortunately, as I started following the highway it climbed up a mountain back into the clouds, making it impossible to leave the valley. I turned around and proceeded to find the airport south of Caliente that was uncontrolled and had lights that were activated by keying the radio microphone on the local UNICOM frequency. Unfortunately, I had no electrical power and no radios that would give me that option.

When the lightning flashed, I saw an airfield running in an east-west direction with two red approach lights on the east end. I moved back over to the left side of the aircraft and fastened my lap belt and then approached the runway from the east. With the gear and flaps down, my approach speed was about ninety miles per hour, but I noticed I was traveling across the lights of the town at a very high speed and figured that the wind was coming from behind me. At about 500 feet above the ground, I proceeded over the runway and then turned 180 degrees to approach the airfield into the wind. My ground speed immediately reduced considerably, which made me believe there were very high winds coming out of the northeast.

Without the red approach lights on the opposite end of the runway, I decided to put the plane down in the rolling hills because I had fifty gallons of fuel on board; if I struck an aircraft or hangar on the runway and created a spark, that Aztec would have gone up in flames. I secured all the electrical switches in the cockpit as a precaution, slowed the aircraft just above a stall speed with full power to the engines and hoping to keep the wings level, and waited for the aircraft to touch the ground. It was like landing in an inkwell. The last thing I remember was the wheels touching down. And because I'd forgotten to latch my shoulder harness (separate from the lap belt), my head hit the instrument panel, and I was knocked unconscious.

I awoke after about fifteen minutes with sleet hitting the left side of my face because the emergency window had blown out. I was surprised the aircraft was still level and there was no fire, even though fuel was running out of the wings. The first thing I did was to determine my injuries. I found my right ankle was twisted over 180 degrees and apparently shattered. I believe this was because, when I touched down, I felt I was sliding to the left and locked my foot to the right rudder to correct the drift. My head hit the instrument panel, knocking the altimeter completely through the panel and causing my concussion. I also hit my throat on the control wheel, ripping open a large gash near my vocal cords. Because the temperature was near freezing, my blood coagulated and kept me from bleeding to death.

I removed the back seat and jammed it into the gaping hole in the pilot's window to stop the sleet and cold air from coming in then crawled into the back and tried to keep as warm as possible, sleeping on and off for about eight hours.

About 6:00 a.m. the next morning, I heard the sound of voices. Apparently, a couple of kids had lost a spare tire off their pickup the night before and came back to find it. I tried to call out, but my voice was too weak due to the injury. And after the kids found their tire, they disappeared over a ridge. Because I had no electrical power, I had been unable to squawk an emergency code on my transponder before I crashed.

There was an emergency locator transmitter that was located in the tail section and was activated by a gravitational force of three g's or greater and will send out a signal for up to four days. But I decided to leave the aircraft and look for help, even though help could be on the way if the transmitter was working. Because the cabin door was jammed, I crawled out the emergency window and noticed it was still storming, with temperatures below forty degrees Fahrenheit. I saw that the two engines had curled under the wings due to the full power stall impact that later was determined to be twenty-five g's. But because there was minimal forward speed, the cabin, which was reinforced with stainless steel, was completely intact. That was probably what saved my life, and it was because, when I was teaching flying, I always told my students to land into the wind if possible because forward speed kills.

Due to my broken ankle, I started crawling on my hands and knees like an animal in the direction I thought was toward Highway 93, about a mile away. After a while, the road noise got weaker. Then I realized I was going in the wrong direction because, when the plane hit the ground, it had spun around 180 degrees. With the overcast skies and no sun to go by, I'd gotten disoriented and thought east was west. I crawled up and down rolling hills for about a mile until I reached a ridge and saw the highway but had to cross a stream and a barbed wire fence to get there.

I finally got up to the highway and started waving my arms to stop a vehicle. But because of the heavy sleet and rain, nobody saw me. In fact, a semi damn near ran me over. Then a pickup swerved around me and stopped. He backed up and got out and said he'd thought I was a dead animal on the side of the road. As soon as I saw him, my adrenalin stopped pumping and my body collapsed. Even though he was in his sixties, he somehow lifted me up and put me into his pickup. I tried to tell him I'd spent the night in a crashed aircraft and was extremely cold. So, he turned his heater up full blast and raced to the hospital in the town of Panaca.

The nurses undressed me and wrapped me in layers of blankets to raise my body temperature. As soon as the doctor finished immobilizing my leg and bandaging my wounds, I was flown to Las Vegas in the "Flight for Life" helicopter to Valley Hospital. The weather was still overcast, with blowing sleet, and I thought, after saving my own life now, I had to rely on someone else's flying experience. I wasn't sure which was worse.

After a bumpy, painful forty-five-minute flight, we finally landed at the helipad on the roof of the hospital. I was immediately taken to surgery and had steel plates and screws put in my ankle and sixty-four stitches put in my face and neck, and I had my broken jaw wired for the third time. I don't know how I crawled a mile from the plane to the highway, but my body was so weak I lay in the hospital bed for eight days without moving; the mind has incredible power.

After the National Transportation Safety Board found the aircraft that afternoon they came by the hospital a few days later to find out just what the hell had happened during that flight. I told them that, if anything could go wrong, it would go wrong (Murphy's Law), and I should have landed at Tonopah while it was still daylight and clear. The inspectors inspected the wreckage and electrical system and found both alternators and regulators were working properly, even though the lightning drained all my power. They also realized I had thirteen thousand hours of flying time and had flown combat missions in Vietnam. And since nobody was killed and no property was damaged besides the aircraft, they had more important cases to attend to. On the way out, one inspector said, of all the aircraft accidents in Nevada during 1982, I was the only one to come out alive, and good luck with the rest of my life.

During the following year while I was recovering, I decided to sue

Vindar Aviation and Darrell Scott for falsely representing an aircraft that was said to be in good condition. Unfortunately, the judge ruled for the defendant, saying that nothing could be proved, and it was ultimately the pilot in command's decision to take the flight. It seemed the more experience a pilot had, the more people depended on his ability to fly any aircraft, regardless of the condition.

There is a saying. "There are old pilots, and there are bold pilots, but there are no old bold pilots." Well, I think I proved that statement to be wrong. During the accident, I had lost my peripheral vision due to the impact of my head hitting the instrument panel. That prevented me from passing my flight physical, consequently causing me to lose my commercial pilot's license. I also couldn't attend my navy reserve meetings. So, I talked our yeoman into putting me on an administrative hold for six months until I was able to make the meetings. I had nineteen years in the navy and only needed one more for retirement eligibility. If it wasn't for that yeoman, I would have been discharged and lost everything; that was a very lucky time in my life.

A couple years after the accident, I saw a friend of mine, Jim, who traded old military aircraft for static displays planes. He traded a World War II A-26 for a 1941 Navy Stearman bi-wing training aircraft that had been sitting in the air force museum in Dayton, Ohio, for two years and talked me into helping him retrieve it. We flew from Santa Rosa, California, to Dayton, Ohio; rented a pickup; and then towed the disassembled Stearman to a private airfield nearby.

After attaching the wings and control cables, we put gas, oil, and a battery in it, and it fired up. I taxied around for a while, trying to wear the rust off the brakes. But they kept sticking, so I decided to take it up for a test flight. Everything seemed to be working OK. But when I touched down, the left brake locked and I spun around like a top, somehow managing to keep from flipping over.

Jim loaded an extra cylinder in the baggage compartment and decided to ride back to Santa Rosa with me, adding 250 pounds more than I'd anticipated. As we approached our first fuel stop, the 220-horsepower engine started sputtering, and when we got on the ground, I found dried fuel film in the fuel tanks.

On the way over the southern Rocky Mountains, I let Jim read the map. But he took me up the wrong canyon, which was 2,000 feet higher than I expected. With the extra weight, the plane wasn't going to clear the pass, and the canyon was too narrow to turn around so I stalled that Stearman into some trees just short of a lake at 10,500 feet. With only a few scratches, we hiked up to a highway and caught a ride to an airport in Durango and then flew back to California.

Jim wanted that plane so badly that we drove back to Colorado to the scene of the crash a week later, only to find the wreckage had been removed. We found out the local sheriff was holding the evidence, waiting for someone to claim the unregistered airplane. Jim went to the sheriff's office to inquire about the plane. But when they saw the scratches on his face, they started to get suspicious. Well, we got the hell out of town before they caught us. I always seemed to get into trouble when someone offered me money, so I just had to say no.

I tried selling airplanes in Sacramento but didn't get along with the owner. And while I was there, I found a 1972 Cessna 177RG Cardinal that had had a gear-up landing two years earlier. I made the owner an offer and then pulled the engine out for overhaul, installed a radio package, and reupholstered the interior. I flew the airplane to Lincoln Airport just north of Sacramento to have the retractable gear adjusted and decided to set up an aircraft-selling business there with another pilot.

After the gear was checked I flew my Cardinal to Sonoma to show it to my mother and sister. I made a low pass over the Sonoma runway, pulled up, and lowered the landing gear—only to discover the nose gear wouldn't come down. I flew back to Lincoln, shut the engine down so as not to damage the propeller, and landed in a cow pasture. A mechanic friend of mine came out, and as I sat on the tail, he used a crowbar and got the nose gear down. Then I took off for the airport and put it in a hangar before the police arrived. The only damage was to the skin, which cost about $1,000 including repairing the nose gear problem.

I finally sold the Cardinal and took a C-172 Skyhawk in on trade and made a $5,000 profit.

CHAPTER 6

BACK TO SCHOOL

After a year of my partner not pulling his weight, I sold my mobile home in Lincoln; took my airplane and Hobie Cat; moved to Kenwood, California, to live with my mother; and enrolled at Sonoma State University to study geology. It worked out well for both of us. My mother lived alone and needed work done on the house, and I needed a place to live while going to school.

The first year was very difficult because of all the science courses and the lapsed time since I'd been in school. The worst course was calculus—until one weekend I took the instructor up for a flying lesson and found out he had two left feet with no coordination. My outlook toward him changed. I wasn't intimidated anymore and passed his course; it was all relative.

One weekend, I took my Hobie Cat sailboat to Bodega Bay and ventured out toward the Farallon Islands by myself. When I was about five miles off shore, I realized how big that ocean was and how small my Hobie cat was and decided to turn back. The swells were so high at times the horizon would completely disappear. And then I was hit by a sneak wave that almost capsized that Hobie cat. I thought, *I damn near killed myself in an airplane. So, what the hell am I doing out here in this little sixteen-foot sail boat?* I managed to get back to the harbor just before dark.

I spent a year and a half at Sonoma State and then transferred to Humboldt State near Eureka, California, because they had a more extensive geology program. I sold my C-172; bought a twenty-six-foot RV trailer; gave my Hobie cat to my niece; and towed my RV to a trailer court in Trinidad, California, to finish my studies. Humboldt is a laid-back school, with the geology teachers looking like hippies, wearing long hair and still smoking pot.

After a year and a half, I went on a six-week final course in the summer of '89 to Mazurka Canyon near Independence, California, with twenty other students who got A's in the classroom but couldn't tell east from west in the field. I brought my RV with me, while the rest of the students slept in their tents on the ground; it was nice to be older and wiser.

Toward the end of the field trip, I rented a C-206 six-passenger plane and flew my classmates over Mazurka Canyon to look at the outcrops we were mapping eventually, getting an A in the course. And that was the last time I flew an aircraft.

One night after a few beers, a twenty-three-year-old botanist who came down from school to give us a crash course on the local flora followed me to my RV, where she lost her virginity. I'm sure she didn't just come down to study the plants because, every time I would ask her, she would look at me and just smile. Our relationship lasted until I moved to Reno, Nevada, to work in the gold mines, and she went to Oregon to work for the forest service. I guess it wasn't to be.

I worked the summer and fall of 1990 in Nevada and met Tilly Botti at the Moana tennis courts. He was a seventy-year-old, retired air force reserve lieutenant colonel who made his money buying and selling land and loaning money on first deeds of trust. He said while I was out in the field working to save my money, he would get me started in the loan business. My first loan was for $15,000, receiving a monthly check of $250. I would get very nervous every time the guy would miss a payment. But Tilly said, "Don't worry. You'll get used to it. And besides, the property is worth twice the loan." His favorite thing was to show everybody the checks he would get in the mail every day.

It was December 1, 1990, so I packed my bags and drove down to

Travis AFB near Sacramento, California, but missed a flight to Hickam AFB, Hawaii, because all of the seventy-three seats were taken by active-duty personnel on vacation with their kids. I managed to catch a C-5A Galaxy that was going to Norton AFB near Riverside, California, unannounced, and there were only two passengers on board.

The best way to Hickam AFB isn't always a straight flight. Sometimes, you have to fly to lesser traveled bases to avoid the crowd, which will get you there quicker than waiting around Travis AFB. I spent a couple of days at Norton AFB because of the Desert Storm outbreak in Saudi Arabia, causing most of the C-141 and C-5A aircraft to have sensitive cargo on board, where no passengers were allowed. While I was on base, I met Anthony Wolfe, an eighty-two-year-old, retired army major trying to get to India, where he lived. I also met Don Paul, a retired navy enlisted man who claimed he was a writer and produced survival technique books.

A KC-10 tanker was departing March AFB for Hickam AFB the next day, so Don drove Anthony and me to the base in his camper, which was so littered with junk there was barely enough room for the three of us. That night, I played tennis with Don, who also claimed to have been a professional tennis player at one time and had a 110-mile per hour serve. But I eventually beat him because he was out of shape.

The next morning we went to the passenger terminal to check on the flight, but nobody was there. I checked with base operations, and they said no aircraft were scheduled to depart for Hickam that day. Later that morning a sergeant showed up and told us that a KC-10 was departing for Hickam in an hour, and there were just enough seats available for the fifteen of us waiting in the terminal. It was a fairly new aircraft, quiet and comfortable, taking about five hours to get to Hickam AFB.

Due to Desert Storm, the airport at Hickam was very busy and unorganized, with passengers sleeping all around the terminal. We rented a car for twenty-five dollars, and Don gave us a tour of the island, including Pali Lookout, Pearl Harbor, Old Town, and so on.

Later that evening, Anthony and I got a room at the BOQ, but it had only one bed. So, I took a shower and went back to the passenger terminal with Anthony and stayed in the USO facility and spent the night reading. The next day, Anthony and I went to Waikiki by bus for sixty cents and were dropped off near the Royal Hawaiian Hotel that Anthony hadn't seen since 1938. Then we walked along Ohua Street owned by Jamie Rich, but only about a half a dozen original houses remained; the rest were hotels and apartments.

Anthony lived with Mary Aster, the actress, and her daughter, who was fathered by John Barrymore, and also with Doris Duke, the heir to the R. J. Reynolds Company but said she was very unpredictable and a little psychotic. She had a beautiful house on Diamond Head that was visible from Waikiki.

Anthony was dying from lymphacide, and his visit around town was the most enjoyable day he'd had in twenty years. After returning to Hickam, we checked into a visiting officers' quarters, which was a two-bedroom house with kitchen and laundry room for $10 each. While Anthony was washing his clothes for the first time in two weeks (he traveled light), I walked to the O club to watch *Monday Night Football*, where I got free hot dogs and chili and fifty-cent beer.

CHAPTER 7

AUSTRALIA 1990

Saddam Hussein and operation Desert Shield interrupted the flight schedules in and out of Hickam. The furthest south I could go on a MAC flight was Guam, so I purchased a ticket to Sydney from SATO in the passenger terminal. If I wanted to hang around Hickam for a couple of weeks, I might have caught a flight to Richmond Royal Australian Air Force Base in Australia. But for $435, I decided to go commercial. I relaxed the next day at the Hickam pool near billeting, swam a mile, and worked on my tan. I said goodbye to Anthony and wished him well with his health and then departed Honolulu International Airport for Sydney, arriving eleven hours later.

I had a visa for Australia that was good for six months, with multiple entries up to three years. After arriving in Sydney, I took a bus for A$2.50 (US$2) to the CB Hotel in the center of town and checked in for A$25 (US$20) a night, which included a community bathroom, shower, and television room.

The city reminded me of Los Angeles, hot and smoggy and spread out, with a lot of traffic. I spent the first day navigating on the subways, which for A$1 would take you anywhere in the city. The next day, I went to Kings Cross, similar to Greenwich Village, where I was told cars were sold by visitors leaving the country and ranged from A$500 to A\$3,000. But I decided to wait for a while because the train and bus system seemed to be very efficient.

I went to the Rocks area to visit the Geological and Mining Museum. But it was being restored and wouldn't be open for another year, at which time it would be the largest geological museum in the world. I found a very popular pub across the street, where I drank 6 percent stout and talked with the local patrons. Later that evening, the place got so crowded people moved out into the street and drank their beer.

The next day while standing in line at the Thomas Cook Exchange to cash some traveler's checks, I met Ali Jefferies, a thirty-seven-year-old schoolteacher from Alberta, Canada. We visited the Sydney Aquarium, which had a glass tube you walked through and saw sharks and stingrays swimming over and under you. Then we went to the observatory because she was interested in astronomy. Ali had been traveling abroad for about four months, and Australia and New Zealand were her last stops.

The following day, we took a two-hour train ride to Katoomba, where we hiked through the Blue Mountains, a limestone canyon similar to our Grand Canyon but smaller and named after the eucalyptus trees that create a blue hue in the morning mist. Ali had picked up a cold in the Far East and passed it on to me by using my water bottle; next time I'd know better. That afternoon, we visited the Sydney Museum of Natural History and studied the Aborigines and origin of man and then went for a swim at a fifty-meter pool near the main train station.

The next day, after Ali left for New Zealand, I visited the Pioneer Mining Exploration and obtained some geology contacts in Perth and Kalgoorlie for possible employment.

Well, I'd seen enough of Sydney. So I bought a ticket on the V/Line train south to Melbourne, Victoria, for A\$116, first class. It was the middle of December, and the outside temperature is above a hundred degrees Fahrenheit, but the train was air-conditioned, making the twelve-hour trip very comfortable. The conductor suggested I go to Adelaide and then north by bus to Cooper Pedy to visit the opal mines and then to Darwin to visit the diamond mines.

I arrived in Melbourne in the evening and checked into the John Spencer, a remodeled hotel, for A\$29 per night, including breakfast. The city and weather reminded me of San Francisco, wet and cold because of the Bass Strait and semi-friendly people conservatively dressed.

A friend of mine in Reno suggested I contact Noel Dicker in Launceston, Tasmania, to see about playing some tennis. Noel told me to visit Kooyong Lawn Tennis Club, located about thirty minutes by train north of Melbourne. The club was established in 1850 with grass courts and was the original home of the Australian Open, located now in Melbourne Park with hard courts. I played doubles at Kooyong and met John Law, a retired civil engineer who invited me to his house for dinner and to meet his wife, Thelma. John then invited me to spend Christmas and New Years at his summer cottage in Hals Gap in the Grampians National Park with his wife and their thirty-year-old daughter, who was coming down from Sydney for a week.

I went back to Melbourne for a couple of days but had trouble meeting people. Then I went to the Loaded Dog Pub Brewery and met a girl who told me I should slow down and relax and enjoy their country.

I took the train to Hals Gap and was met by Christine, who drove me to their cottage. When I got out of the car, I presented John with a bottle of Grant's scotch and a five-pound ham. And can you believe it? He presented me with the same thing.

Peter's backyard was like my own animal park, with koala bears in the trees, a kookaburra bird that came for dinner every night, and cockatoos and kangaroos everywhere. John and I played tennis each morning, went for hikes with his wife in the afternoon, and drank scotch and told jokes in the evening.

Then their thirty-year-old daughter Hilary arrived, and the mood changed. At first she was very cold and self-centered. But after a few days and some crazy times with her and her family, she started to warm up. One day, we went hiking and saw some emus and later had lunch with some kangaroos. Christine was always suggesting that Hilary and I get together and once told her daughter she would like a grandchild.

We all got pleasantly drunk Christmas night and wound up in their pool, all of which was on videotape. After John and Christine went to bed, Hilary said she wanted to have oral sex with me. Well, being that her parents had locked me out of the house, I was forced to spend the night with Hilary in the outside guest room. We'd had a little too much to drink that night, so the sex was not that enjoyable. The next night after everyone had gone to bed, I snuck out to the guest house and had a very memorable night with Hilary, giving her multiple orgasms.

Hals Gap was like Yosemite Valley; there was a magnificent waterfall called McKenzie and a sliver of rock called "the Nerve Test." You could walk out on it, but it dropped off several hundred feet on either side.

One day when John and I were in town at a pub, he introduced me to the game of cricket that was on television. It was a very interesting game that required a lot of patience and sometimes lasted for days.

The holidays were over, and Hilary went back to Sydney. So, after helping John work around his cottage, I decided to head west toward Perth. Emotions were high as I departed, as John and Christine thought they were never going to see me again.

I took a midnight train to Adelaide in South Australia and sat/slept for eight hours with a young Swedish girl who was going to Perth as an exchange student. I took an old electric tram that was built in the early 1900s to Glenelg on the coast outside of Adelaide, where, for $40, I spent the night in a motel that was next to the Pier and Pine, a popular pub that had a bucket of shrimp and chips for $6.

The next day after a little sun and a swim in the Indian Ocean, I went to Adelaide and bought a ticket to Perth on the Indian Pacific Train for $400 and was assigned to a berth with a foldaway bed and a sink but a community shower. Every morning, the steward would bring me a cup of tea with cream, and then certain bell combinations would signal me for either breakfast, lunch, or dinner in a very elegant dining car. I met some pretty schoolteachers in the club car, where we drank great beer, played cards, and had good conversation because I was the only one on board from the United States. The trip took three days crossing the Nullarbor, which means "no trees" and extends across a limestone plateau in Western Australia. There is a section of track that is absolutely straight for 438 kilometers. And as desolate as that country was, every once in a while, you would see an abandoned car that had been there for decades.

We stopped for fuel in Kalgoorlie, which I wanted to visit. But

I couldn't get off the train because my ticket was for Perth. I arrived in Perth on the morning of January 6, 1991, and then took a local train to downtown and found the Hotel Regatta for A$32 per night, including breakfast. The weather was magnificent, with clear skies and temperatures in the mideighties. I went to the Royal Perth Lawn and Tennis Club and met John Daniels, a dentist who gave me some geology contacts in town for employment.

The next day, I took a train to Fremantle, a quiet little town on the coast about thirty kilometers south of Perth. I went for a swim at the Fremantle Pool, where some Americans were training for a championship meet. Among them were Janet Evans and Matt Biondi, who later set new world records at the Superdrome in Perth. Then I stopped by the Fremantle Lawn and Tennis Club and met Damian Shanks, who invited me to come back Saturday to play with the club members. Later that day, I found the Sail and Anchor Pub, where you cooked your own steak and drank 6 percent stout with great company.

I tried contacting some geology companies the next day but was told this was a bad time of the year, both for vacations and because a 35 percent gold tax had just been levied on the companies. As a result, they were either shutting down or consolidating.

Every night, I would go to the Mangoes Bar next to my hotel, where I was pampered by Michelle, Michaelia, and Haley, three beautiful bartenders. We would tell jokes and talk about the differences between the Yanks and the Aussies. One day, I found Robertson Park and played lawn tennis with a group of businessmen, who invited me out for dinner that night. Taking my racquet with me opened a lot of doors. The businessmen told me about a nude beach. So, the next day I took a bus to Swanbourne, where I worked on my complete tan and met some very friendly and easygoing people.

The Royal Perth Yacht Club in Fremantle was having a regatta, and I saw Dennis Connors from San Diego who was in third place out of sixty entries in a world race sailing an Etchells 22 Class boat. Fremantle had a predictable wind they called "the doctor" that blew every afternoon; it was good for sailing but not so good for playing tennis.

The next day, Damian picked me up in Perth, and we went to the

Fremantle Lawn and Tennis Club for the day. I met Brian the manager and his pretty daughter. Brian told me to visit Roxby Downs, a gold mining town and then go south to Albany via Margaret River. The tennis club organized doubles matches, and every hour, a bell rang and you were paired up with someone else. But at two o'clock everyone stopped playing tennis and had tea and pastries. I wondered, Did they do this while fighting a war?

While walking around Perth, I noticed that the Aborigines were very lazy and an unproductive race because the Australians had taken away their land and incentive to work by giving them welfare money. I was sitting in the Hay Street Mall reading a *USA Today* when a clock tower struck on the hour, and two figures came out and started jousting—only in Australia. Well, it was January 15, and the paper said Saddam wanted to go to war. Given my current location, the naval reserves would have a hard time locating me if they decided to recall.

I bought a ticket for Kalgoorlie for $53 on the Prospector, a comfortable eighty-five-kilometer per hour, two-car diesel train that reminded me of an airline. During the seven-hour trip, I was served a delicious lunch with a bottle of Darling Vineyards claret. I arrived in Kalgoorlie at four in the afternoon and, for A$34, checked into the Old Australian Hotel, which was very clean and run by a young couple, Ted and Barbara from Adelaide.

The next day, I talked with Andrew Extract of the Department of Mines, who was an engineer from the United States who'd married an Australian. He said that I should obtain a work permit and then find a job that didn't compete with other geologists but that it seemed very unlikely because of the 35 percent gold tax that had been incorporated January 1, 1991.

I then went to the school of mines. The school had a total enrollment of seventy-five students, of which 10 percent were postgraduates. The professor told me that, if I enrolled in the graduate program, which would take two years, there was a good chance I could find employment in Australia. I told him I'd think about it.

That evening, I went to the Palace Hotel for a cook-your-own T-bone steak and found a cute bartender serving beer wearing nothing but a G-string. I went to Hay Street and talked with the hookers, who said they charge US$60 for a half hour and knew all about the Mustang Ranch in Reno, Nevada. I had a few beers with Ted and Barbara on their balcony that night and was joined by a couple from England. But because they considered Americans to be very arrogant, we didn't get along very well.

The next morning. Ted drove me to an outcrop six kilometers southeast of town believed to be the second oldest rocks in the world. The rocks contained 50 percent magnesium, 30 percent quartz and 20 percent hematite and limonite and appeared to have been partially metamorphosed, cooked, tilted, and then uplifted.

The following morning, I had breakfast served to me on my balcony. And after saying goodbye, I took the Prospector back to Perth and noticed a pipeline following the tracks for about 650 kilometers. I found out later that it was the only fresh water supply to Kalgoorlie.

I hired (rented) a Ford Laser GT from Bayswater car rental for A$37 per day with unlimited mileage. It was a five-speed, five-door hatchback; got forty kilometers per gallon on the highway; and had the steering wheel on the wrong side. I went to the Royal Automobile Club and picked up some maps before heading out of town, having trouble staying on the left side of the road. After a few close calls, I finally got on the open road and cranked it up to 110 kilometers miles per hour (68 miles per hour), which was the maximum speed limit.

My first stop was Bunbury, a small fishing town, where I found a room at the Captain Bunbury Hotel for A$15 per night that had a bistro with great food. The next morning, I walked down to the beach and saw people wading in the water taking pictures and touching a school of dolphins. This ritual went back fifty years to a time when a local Australian woman who lived near the estuary would beat a rake on the water and then feed the dolphins. As many as fifteen at a time would swim to her. One dolphin I saw had cuts on his body and a ripped jaw, probably from a shark attack. The people in town were very relaxed and happy, and even though they didn't have much money, they weren't stressed out like the Americans.

I headed south the next day along the coastline and stopped at

Meelup Beach for a swim. But I got stung all over my body by small man o' war jellyfish. It took vinegar to relieve the pain. I stayed at a hostel in Dunsborough for $21 and shared a room with three other guys, where no smoking or drinking of alcohol was allowed. Betty, who ran the hostel, gave me a few names of wineries nearby. So, the following day, I stopped at Cape Clairault Winery and met the owners, Ian and Ani Lewis. Ian had been a geologist for twenty years but had decided to start his own wine business in 1981 and was doing quite well. He gave me a bottle of cabernet, and I told him I would send him a bottle of wine from Napa Valley when I got home. After saying goodbye, I stopped at Cozy Corner Beach to work on my complete tan.

I heard that Saddam fired the first shot, so President Bush went to war trying to assassinate that son of a bitch. It seemed as though we went after Iraq, and Iraq went after Israel, making it a three-way battle. So, I figured I'd stay in Australia until the crisis was over just in case the United States tried to call back the retired reserves.

I arrived in Augusta where the Indian and Southern Oceans met, marked by a lighthouse at latitude 34.22 south and longitude 115.08 east. I picked up a couple of hitchhikers from England and scared the hell out of them with my driving because I was either going too fast or was on the wrong side of the highway. They finally asked to be dropped off in the middle of nowhere and said they would rather walk the rest of the way—no sense of humor.

I finally got to Albany at the bottom of Western Australia and checked into the Premier Hotel for A$21. When I walked into the pub, it was standing room only. The people were very friendly and kept buying me beers as long as I talked about America. Then at exactly twelve midnight, the placed closed, and everyone moved out to the street with their beers. The weather was similar to Oregon, cold and foggy, and since there wasn't much to do here, I decided to go back to Perth.

I drove back on the inland freeway, which took only four hours and checked back into the Hotel Regatta. Since I didn't think I was going to do any geology work here, I sent my extra bag and equipment back to the United States for A$40; it would take about two months to arrive, traveling by air, sea, or whatever. After more tennis and swimming, I called the Richmond RAAF near Sydney and learned flights were leaving for the United States every Wednesday and Friday. So, I bought a ticket on Australian Airlines for A$280; the flight would depart January 24.

That night, I went to Tracks Bistro near the train terminal for beer and a steak and met Jodi and her mother, who proceeded to drink me under the table; those Aussies could sure hold their liquor.

Australia Day, a busy flying weekend, was coming up on January 26. So, the aircraft refuellers decided to go on strike, leaving me in Perth for a while. One night, I tried to get a better deal on a hotel, but all I got was a soft bed in a hot room full of mosquitoes; I never learn.

I met Ely Quartermaine, president of the Royal Perth Yacht Club, who invited me to crew in a regatta in a thirty-foot sailboat on the Swan River. There were five other crew members, including the owner's daughter, who wouldn't leave me alone during the race. I ran the main sheet, and despite all the confusion on board, we managed to come in second out of six other boats in our class. Then "*The Doctor*" came up on schedule and capsized two boats. After the race trophies were awarded, speeches were made, and beer was flowing; as usual, they all wanted to know about America.

Later that day, I went to the Sail and Anchor Pub in Fremantle and was introduced to traditional bitters brewed on the premises; it contained 9 percent alcohol and almost tasted like wine. A man came into the bar with a video camera and said he was doing a story on pubs in Western Australia. But as I watched him, I realized he was a private investigator filming an individual in the bar who didn't notice him because he was very intoxicated. The women here were very polite and easy to talk to and were attracted to Yanks because the Aussie men treated them like a commodity with no respect. They were also full breasted and showed them off by wearing loose-fitting bras while walking down the street.

One afternoon on the train to Fremantle, I met a girl from Ireland who was backpacking around Australia. She showed me how to condense my personal effects so I didn't have to carry as much weight around on my back. After arriving in Fremantle, I tried to check into the New Orleans Bourbon and Beefsteak Pub but was told the only room left had to be shared with three girls. When I opened the door, they were all sitting around in their underwear. Dori was from Canada and in her late twenties. Olivia and her sister were from Melbourne, nineteen and twenties years of age respectively. We shared bunk beds and dressed in front of each other for three days without any problems. I guess they felt comfortable around an older yank.

One morning after breakfast at the Carriage Shop, I played some tennis and then swam and got some sun at the aquatic park. I had a steak and salad that night at the Beefsteak Bar and was entertained by a trio who imitated the Mamas and the Papas all for only five dollars. The bar used to be a headquarters for drug dealers before the Americas Cup arrived in 1987. Now it was being remodeled and was set to be a very clean and popular place by 1992.

The refueling strike was over, so I left Perth the next day on Australian Airlines for a six-hour flight to Sydney, running into a storm over Adelaide that towered over forty thousand feet. But it cleared up before we got to Sydney. The meals and service on Australian Airlines were much better than on airlines in the United States. I checked back into the CB Hotel in Sydney, located on Pitt Street, and discovered, after having traveled around Australia, that Sydney was not as clean as it had appeared the first time I'd arrived. So, my favorite city was Perth.

The next morning, I called Richmond RAAF and discovered that a flight was departing for Norton AFB, California, in three hours—egad. I checked out of the hotel and went to the train station but didn't have enough time to buy a ticket because of the long lines at the window. I fought my way through the crowds at the station, and just as I got on the train, the doors closed behind me. After riding for an hour and a half, I arrived at Riverton and had to change trains. But since I didn't have a ticket, I had to stand in line again—only to find out that the other train was leaving in two minutes. Believe it or not, just as I got on, the train the doors closed behind me again. This one was an old wooden train built in the early 1900s, and it didn't go over forty miles per hour making stops every ten minutes.

I arrived in Richmond fifteen minutes before my flight was supposed to depart, and the only taxi available had just left the train station.

About five minutes later, the taxi arrived. But a woman asked if she could share it with me and drop her off along the way. Well, I finally arrived at the base five minutes after takeoff time. When I went to the terminal to check in, nobody was there. After tracking down the proper personnel, I was told the time they had given me over the phone was the check-in time, and the aircraft wasn't due to take off for another two hours.

After paying a A$10 customs fee and buying a US$3 meal ticket, we took off in a C-141 Star Lifter on a five-hour flight to Pago Pago in American Samoa, gaining a day crossing over the international dateline. When we got off the plane in Pago Pago, the humidity was 95 percent, and within fifteen minutes, your clothes were soaking wet. A hurricane had passed through the island last year, but buildings were already rebuilt, and the trees were growing back again.

After a couple of hours unloading and loading equipment and refueling, we departed on a six-hour flight for Hickam, Hawaii. The crew had to stay in Hawaii for sixteen hours to rest, so I spent the day swimming, doing my laundry, and shopping. We left Hickam at midnight the next day, arriving at Norton AFB near Riverside, California, at four o'clock in the morning. When the door of the plane opened, the temperature was about forty degrees and raining, and there I was in a polo shirt and shorts. While I was in Australia, California received the worst freeze in fifteen years, and it had been raining for two months, flooding most of the southern state.

I checked in at the terminal. A B-727 was departing for Travis AFB, carrying flight crews back east to pick up C-130s for the Gulf War. It was a contracted plane from New York owned by Trump Airlines and had plush leather seats with telephones and friendly stewardesses, who were intrigued by my dark tan and geological trip around Australia.

I called my mother, who met me at the terminal at Travis. But I decided next time I'd leave my car at the base for five dollars a week so I didn't have to rely on anybody. Flying space available was OK if you were a bachelor and had time to sit around the passenger terminals and weren't on a schedule; you never knew when or where the next flight was going.

CHAPTER 8

CHILE

After working the summer in Nevada, I left on December 28, 1992, and drove to Travis AFB and caught a C-5 to Andrews AFB, Maryland. It was cold and rainy at Andrews. So, while waiting for a flight south, I found some indoor tennis courts on base for a good workout. The next day I caught a C-9 medivac flight to Charleston AFB, South Carolina, via Norfolk NAS, Virginia, and Pope AFB, North Carolina, picking up and dropping off patients.

The base at Charleston was cleaner, more organized, and less crowded than Andrews, with plenty of space in the bachelors' quarters, including a VIP suite for only eight dollars a night, including a wet bar and kitchen. The weather was a little warmer. So, one evening, I went to the outdoor tennis courts and picked up a game with one of the base personnel. Because of the New Year holiday routine, no flights were scheduled for a few days. So, I spent New Year's Eve at the noncommissioned officers' club drinking forty-eight-ounce draft beer for two dollars with all the chicken and potato salad I could eat.

Thursday morning, January 2, 1993, I went to the passenger terminal and talked with a reserve sergeant, who signed me up on a flight to Howard AFB, Panama, even though I was still in the retired reserves and couldn't fly out of the Continental United States until I reached age sixty and fully retired. I departed that morning on a C-141, and upon arrival at Howard, the temperature was ninety degrees, with humidity around 85 Percent, my kind of weather. I took a three-mile cab ride to Rodman Panama Canal Naval Station for two dollars and checked into a two-bedroom suite overlooking the O club pool for fifteen dollars per night. I swam at the pool and worked on my tan during the day and then had a couple of cocktails at the club that night, along with a shrimp dinner, wine, and cognac for twenty-five dollars.

The next day I rented a Daihatsu for twenty-five dollars and visited the Miraflores Locks at the Panama Canal and then went shopping in Panama City, where I bought sixty-dollar Gucci polo shirts for ten dollars each. I got lost trying to get back to the base that night and wound up in El Charillo, an extremely dangerous part of town, where prisoners were housed in small shacks along the wharf. I finally picked up a Panamanian boy at a gas station, and for a couple of dollars, he helped me navigate across the Bridge of Americas to the naval base.

I went to Howard AFB passenger terminal to sign up for a flight to Chile, and the sergeant asked how I'd gotten to Panama. I told him a reservist in Charleston had put me on a flight. Well, I wasn't supposed to fly outside the United States. However, since I was here, the military was obligated to get me back to the United States. But I was on my own while in South America.

I bought a ticket to Santiago, Chile, via La Paz, Bolivia, for $450 and then spent the rest of the day at the O club swimming and playing tennis. That night, I had a prime rib dinner at the club and then drove to the Tocumen International Airport south of Panama City to catch my flight to Bolivia. I departed on a Lloyd Aero Boliviano B-727 at one o'clock in the morning, arriving at La Paz eight hours later. But when we landed, I felt very dizzy then realized the airport was at four thousand meters (twelve thousand feet) above sea level.

After I checked into the Presidente Hotel downtown, the room steward brought me some tea, which cleared up my head within thirty minutes. Then I found out it was made from cocoa leaves, a derivation of cocaine. That afternoon, I went shopping and met Roberto Mendez, who worked in a tin mine in Potosi during the winter and gave climbing tours in the summer. He spoke fairly good English and was friendly to talk to, so we shopped together. He got me a good deal on an alpaca sweater, gloves, and hat for fifteen dollars that would have cost a hundred dollars in the United States. The next day, I visited Scotty Bruce of Mintec Mining, who said I should go to Chile if I wanted to find work in geology.

I checked into the Crillion Hotel, which Roberto had found for me, for twenty-seven dollars, half the price of the Presidente and more centrally located. The next day, Roberto and I climbed Chacaltaya Mountain, which is 5,600 meters (17,360 feet). After a snowstorm blew through, we could see Illimani, the highest peak in Bolivia at 6,400 meters (19,840 feet). Roberto talked me into chewing some cocoa leaves that he said would increase my energy level. But when the effect wore off, I had the worst headache (withdrawal) and decided never to try it again.

The next day, Roberto and I went to a tin mine near Milluni, 4,600 meters, where miners worked the mine by manual labor, including crushing of the rocks. The miners lived with their families on site and very seldom saw outsiders, let alone an American, but I found them to be very friendly. A cemetery near the mine contained hundreds of graves of miners who had died at young ages over the past fifty years from working in the mine.

As we drove through the mountains, I noticed corn, wheat, potatoes, and other crops being grown at 11,000 feet using irrigation from the higher mountains. We saw llamas and alpacas grazing in the plateaus, the difference being that alpacas were smaller and had softer and finer wool. That afternoon, we climbed to 5,200 meters along treacherous cliffs and slippery rocks to an ice cave that exposed layers of time over thousands of years. On the way down the trail, we saw a gravesite where a Korean motorcyclist lost control three years ago and plunged three thousand feet down the mountain to his death.

The next morning, I woke up to a very pleasant day. So, I decided to check out the tennis club, which was located down the valley in an exclusive area where the temperature was warmer. The Club de Florida had clay courts, but because I was a visitor, I needed a sponsor, and there were no exceptions. So, I guess tennis wasn't to be.

Roberto called me and he, his niece, and I went to Tiwanaku Inca ruins, built in 1580 BC and occupied until AD 133. We also visited the Iglesia de Tiahuanaco, a church built in 1680 that was having the frescos restored by young painters from Argentina. That night, we had dinner together and then went shopping. I bought his niece Elizabeth a beautiful wool sweater for just $3.75; but because they were poor, it was quite a gift for her.

While I was waiting for my flight at the airport the next day, Roberto and his niece came to say goodbye and gave me a commercial box of cocoa tea to take home. I departed La Paz on a Lloyd Aero Boliviano B-727 that took the whole twelve thousand-foot runway to take off, even though we were light on fuel. Our first stop was Arica, Chile, near sea level for fuel and then we flew along the coast to Santiago, the capital of Chile. Chile is like California only upside down, and because it's below the equator, the further south you go, the colder and wetter it gets. The northern part of the country is desert until you reach Santiago, where the water from the Los Andes Mountains has turned the valley into farmland, growing fruits and vegetables. South of Santiago is like Napa Valley, where some of the finest wines from Chile are produced.

On the flight to Santiago, I met David Brown, a Canadian who was meeting a group that had planned a three-week trip through the Amazon. I told him I had a box of cocoa tea to take home, and he advised me to dispose of it because the customs agents might think I was trying to smuggle cocaine. After arriving in Santiago, David and I decided to share a room together at the Hotel Vegas for forty dollars, which was nicer and cheaper than rooming alone.

We had dinner together that night, and while walking through a tourist shopping area, we were attacked by three men trying to pick our pockets. Needless to say, they chose the wrong people. We turned on two of them ready to fight, and they took off running only to send two young boys to try the same thing. My advice is, while in Santiago at night, don't carry large amounts of cash or valuables; in fact, dress down so as not to attract attention.

The next morning after David left with his tour group, I checked out of the Hotel Vegas and found the Hotel Londres just a couple of blocks away for ten dollars a night, including a private bath. I called Bernard Berstien, a geologist referred from the and met with him that afternoon. He said he liked my experience and wanted to take me up to his mine in the Los Andes tomorrow.

That evening, I went for a swim at Piscina de Tupahue Park located on top of a mountain in the southern part of the city. Then I had a nice steak dinner that night at the Radical Restaurant next to my hotel for only seven dollars.

I met with Bernie the next day at his office, and then we departed Santiago in a 4WD Suzuki Samurai, along with Bernie's assistant, Lucio. We spent the night at the Casa Mobile Motel near the base of the Andes, where we were served a magnificent dinner because we were the only ones to check in that night. The motel was situated along the Rio Colorado and was for sale for $40,000 but lacked the tourism traffic. The next morning, we headed up the mountain on a dirt road and across flooded rivers for four hours to the mine site, located 4,100 meters (12,500 feet) above sea level.

Upon arrival, we found the campsite had been destroyed by high winds during the winter, and temporary tents were being used. The mine, which was accessible only four months out of the year, was adjacent to Aconcagua, the tallest mountain in the western hemisphere at 7,000 meters (21,700 feet). The Pimienta Mine, named after the red colored-mountain, contained gold veins running north and south that produced five ounces per ton of ore. There were twenty-five employees working twelve-hour shifts blasting rock and then carrying forty-kilogram (eighty-pound) sacks down the mountain to the campsite. On an average day, the mine produced about two tons of ore, and at $350 per ounce, they grossed about $3,500 if the trucks could get the ore down the mountain to Santiago. Bernie said, if I worked on my Spanish a little more, he would hire me to supervise the men at the mine; I'd think about it.

After we arrived in Santiago the next day, I departed by Tour-Bus, similar to our Greyhound, for $2.25 to Vina del Mar, a resort town on the coast that was the sister city of Sausalito, California. I checked into the El Escorial, a type of family-run bed-and-breakfast, for sixteen dollars a night, a price that included breakfast. The crowd didn't speak English, but we managed to communicate. The beach was similar to beaches in Santa Cruz, California, except for the water, which was polluted because the Chileans dumped raw sewage directly into the ocean.

I got a great haircut at a beauty salon for only $2.50 and then went to the Del Mar Tennis Club and met the tennis pro Javier Gonzales, who worked on my backhand by changing me from a continental to a western grip. He never turned pro because he didn't have the sponsors or the money, which was very unfortunate. I'm sure there is a lot of talent in South America in the same situation. The courts were clay due to the temperate zone and would save ankles and shoes from wearing out. I was using a $50 Wilson racquet that Javier said was worth $150 because American products were hard to acquire in Chile. Later that day, I bought a Hind bathing suit that was cut very small and went to the beach. There, I met some Argentinian schoolteachers who were on summer vacation and wore suits without any tops.

I bought a ticket the next day to Conception on Tour-Bus that included a stereo and a television. The trip took about eight hours, which gave me time to meet the passengers. And with my Spanish improving, I obtained more points of interest to visit. I checked into a hotel downtown for five dollars a night. But it wasn't very clean, so I figured I'd stay in the hostels from now on. I had a sandwich that night at a restaurant and then went downstairs to the saloon and drank beer and sang with the locals.

While shopping the next day, I met a couple of young girls who spent the whole day with me touring the town and sharing cultures. Then I took a Bio-Bio Bus south to Temuco, a clean, quiet town near the University of Chile, where I had lunch and then took the JAC bus to Pucón, near an active volcano. The bus stopped in Villarrica, where it filled up with sunbathers going to a lake resort, and I met Cristina and her girlfriend, who invited me to join them for the day. They were university students and spoke a little English. So, we got along fine, playing volleyball and talking about US and Chilean customs. The lake reminded me of Tahoe in the Sierra Nevada Mountains, cold and clear from the runoff of the Andes Mountains.

I found a clean hostel in town that had a view of the volcano and included breakfast for only sixteen dollars. The next day, I met with Cristina, but she told me her mother and father were very protective and wouldn't let us spend the day together. Apparently, girls from good families remained at home until they were twenty-five years old before they were allowed to marry or go out on their own.

I took the JAC bus to Valdivia and went to some clay courts and hit with Marcelo Mellado, who was the number one ranked junior player in southern Chile. He was only eleven years old and hit a ball better than a sixteen-year-old. I stayed in a hostel that night run by a little old lady for just six dollars, including breakfast. It seemed to be getting cheaper the further south I went.

Well, I was running out of real estate. So, I took a ferry from Ancud to Puerto Montt on the Isla Grande de Chiloe, where I met Gloria Rodriquez, a schoolteacher on vacation from Santiago, who said she would meet me in Santiago after I finished my trip to the south. I found another hostel including breakfast for five dollars a night. At this rate, I could stay down here forever.

The following day I took a bus to Quellón, a fishing village at the south end of the island and found a room at the Hotel Playa and met David Domre, a fisherman who spoke very good English. We got drunk that night on Pisco, a type of liqueur that you have to drink straight because, if mixed with water, it would cause diarrhea and give you one hell of a headache. Then we went to the White House and danced with all the prostitutes until four o'clock in the morning.

The next day, David introduced me to Domingo, the owner of the hotel; his wife, Mogoli; and their two daughters, Carolina and Claudia, who adopted me into their family. My room only cost four dollars a night, and they would wait on me hand and foot. *I've finally found a home away from home*, I thought. Mogoli and her daughters spent the summer with Domingo from March through November, but they lived in Talca, south of Santiago, where the girls went to school; it was a tough life for everyone.

One night, David and I went to a dance, and I met Sonia Hernandez, a twenty-six-year-old aerobics instructor who wanted to get married and go back to the United States with me. I tell you. a single American in Chile wasn't safe.

I bought a ticket on the Transmarchilay Ferry for thirteen dollars that traveled twenty-four hours through high-sea states to Puerto Chacabuco. Because the sun rose at six o'clock in the morning and didn't set until ten o'clock in the evening, I observed some fantastic scenery, including glaciers and active volcanoes. The weather was getting colder and wetter because I was at forty-six degrees south latitude, similar to Vancouver, BC, in the north. I took a five-dollar taxi ride to Puerto Aysén, a picturesque town in the heart of the rain forest that got up to three hundred inches of rain per year. I had a delicious fresh salmon dinner that night and met Edda, a waitress who wanted me to go to Coyhaique tomorrow with her family. Because my Spanish was getting better, we had a great day together in Coyhaique, the last town served by roads in Chile. To get to Punta Arenas, the last town in Chile, you had to go by boat or plane, and after that, the next stop was Antarctica.

It was, February 1, 1993, and before I ran out of time or money, I had better start back to the United States. So, I bought a ticket on Austrial Bus to Chaitén, which included a night's stay en route with dinner and breakfast. The bus was a twelve-passenger minivan because the roads were so narrow that a regular-sized bus would never make the tight curves around the cliffs. The first day, we stopped at Fiordo Queulat for coffee and pastries, and I met Patrick Silva, the owner of the camp. Patrick spoke a little English, so I told Waldo, the bus driver, I was getting off, and he said he would pick me up in a couple of days.

Patrick was in the financing business out of Coyhaique and decided to quit his job and build some cabins in the forest for tourists. So, I paid him forty-two dollars for three days, which included meals, a cabin, and conversation. The next day, Patrick and I and another family who stayed one night went for a hike in the rain forest. Because it rained so much, Patrick furnished everyone with rain coats. Well, I was the only one wearing shorts, and all of a sudden, I felt a stinging sensation on my legs. When I looked down, I saw that my legs were covered with *sanquijuelas* (leeches) that were sucking my blood out. Each time I reached down to remove one, I would yell, "Son of a leech." And everyone would laugh and thought I was crazy for hiking in my shorts.

Patrick said that, if he had the right fishing lures, he could catch a fish similar to the steelhead from Northern California. So, I said I would send him some when I got back to the United States.

About three o'clock on the third day, Waldo showed up in a twelve-seat minivan that had fifteen passengers and a six-month-old baby plus luggage on board. I asked Waldo where I was going to sit, and he said, "No problem." Apparently, someone had bought some furniture. So, I use one of the chairs as the sixteenth seat.

The passengers were a lot of fun. We had a lawyer and his son from Argentina, two students from Santiago, a couple from Germany, a retired schoolteacher, a young couple from Sweden, a highway maintenance supervisor from Chile, and two women and a nursing baby from Chaitén. We spent the first night in Puyuhuapi, where we had a nice dinner and talked about our cultures. The next day, after taking pictures of glaciers and waterfalls, we arrived in Chaitén and had another dinner together. Then Waldo arranged a place for all of us to stay, and that's when I had to get away from the group. I found a hostel for seven dollars including breakfast and met a couple of guys from England, who had been bicycling through Chile for two months.

I departed Chaitén for Quellón on the Transmarchilay. The journey only took six hours, and when I arrived in Quellón, Carolina, Claudia, and David were waiting for me at the pier like they hadn't seen me in a year. I checked back into the Hotel Playa and found that three prostitutes were occupying rooms overlooking the harbor because this was the busy time of the year for the fishermen, and the girls were taking advantage of the situation. They would hang out their windows and whistle at the fishermen as they walked by, trying to negotiate a price for their services.

One night, Domingo's family and I went to see the local folklore music that consisted of a *zampoña* (a type of large flute), two guitars, a violin, a piccolo, and a single drum. The music was very lively and happy, and the girls taught me how to dance, which required using your hips a lot. Then I requested a rock and roll song and showed them how the Americans dance.

I decided to head north and bought a ticket on Tour-Bus. Then after all the hugs and kisses, I took a six-hour ride to Puerto Montt. It was a shipping town, and because Chile had more salmon than Alaska due to its temperate water current, the town shipped salmon all over the world. I got a haircut in town for eight dollars, had a lasagna dinner with a great bottle of Chilean wine, and then walked around listening to street music and bought a cassette tape of Chilean music.

The next day, I bought a ticket on Tour-Bus Cama for forty dollars to Santiago. The ride took ten hours and included all the cocktails you could drink, dinner with wine and dessert, a television with headsets, a seat that reclined, and a bed-and-breakfast the next morning.

When I arrived in Santiago, I called Bernie to tell him about my trip and told him I might be back next year to work for him at his gold mine. I went to the US embassy to inquire about a military flight to Panama but just missed a C-130 that had left that morning. The next plane wasn't due to leave for two weeks. I called Gloria Rodriguez, who I'd met in Ancud. But she was leaving for La Paz, Bolivia, tomorrow and wouldn't be back for two weeks. Then I found a USA Today and saw that the stock I owned had been falling while I'd been away.

Well, with all that bad news, I bought a ticket on Lloyd Aero Boliviano to Panama for $450. The flight left tomorrow, so I spent the day swimming at Piscina de Tupahue. The nightlife here didn't start until midnight and went until six o'clock in the morning. Then the daily workforce got up and the streets were jammed with cars driving like crazy on the wrong side of the road, with no pedestrian right-of-way. The city was founded in 1541 and had a population of 1.5 million people. And because it was inland with no coastal winds, the smog was becoming a concern. Some of the best snow skiing in the world was located just a hundred miles east of Santiago in the Andes near Portillo at 3,000 meters. And because it was south of the equator, the season ran from June through October, with later skiing at higher altitudes.

I went to the airport the next day to check in for my flight and met

Nadia Valcucia, a flight reservation employee, who gave me her address and phone number in case I decided to return to Chile. I'm telling you, if these women found out you were an American and planning to work in Chile, they'd let you know they were available.

I departed Santiago in a B-727 for Panama and got a quick high on a cocktail because our first stop was La Paz at over twelve thousand feet. LAB was a very clean and well maintained airline, with excellent in-flight meals and damn good pilots. During our brief stop in La Paz, the pilots told me that, two years ago, a Paraguay B-727 with 125 passengers had taken off from La Paz in a snowstorm and flown into a mountain near Illimani; and because of the deep snow, it has never been found. Not too many airline or private aircraft are allowed in and out of La Paz because it's the highest airport in the world.

We arrived in Panama at two o'clock in the morning, and because I was tired from the high altitude, I left my Pentax zoom camera under the seat in the plane that continued on to Miami. It wasn't the camera I missed but the undeveloped pictures I would never see again.

The only transportation from the airport was a twenty-dollar cab ride that took me to the Vera Cruz Hotel, which was clean and quiet and cost thirty-three dollars a night. The next morning, I called LAB in Miami and was informed the maintenance crew hadn't found my camera while cleaning the plane. I wasn't surprised. I took a bus to Albrook AFS for forty cents and checked into a VIP suite for eight dollars; there was nothing like the good deals in the military.

I met Enrique (Keke) Prieto at the O club that night. A drug enforcement officer from Bogota, Colombia, he said he was waiting for his partner who was on a sting operation and was overdue by about four hours. If he didn't show up soon, he'd be presumed dead. When I told him I used to fly off an aircraft carrier, he thought I was crazy. But I thought it was nothing compared to the danger he faced everyday as a DEA. If I ever returned to South America and Keke was still alive, I had an open invitation to stay with him and his family in Colombia—hopefully, away from the drug traffic.

The next day after a swim at a fifty-meter pool at Albrook, I caught a C-5 to Dover AFB, Delaware, where the temperature was forty-nine degrees with snow still on the ground when we landed. I took a limo for thirty dollars to Andrews AFB, Maryland, because Dover didn't have any flights going to the West Coast. I played tennis at the indoor courts with Sam Jones and Jim "Bad News" Barns, two Hall of Fame basketball stars and then went to the O club that night and had free hoagie sandwiches and fifty-cent beer during happy hour.

The next morning, the fog was so dense all flights were delayed until noon, when I caught a C-22 (B-727) to Nellis AFB, Las Vegas. Since there were no passengers, I sat in the cockpit with the crew. We had 100-knot headwinds, making our groundspeed only 385 knots, and it took four hours to reach Las Vegas. Nellis was one of the newest bases on the West Coast. I stayed in a suite for nine dollars and then went to the O club and ate and drank all night for free because of a wetting down (promotion) of four lieutenant colonels.

I called my mother in Santa Rosa, California, and found out the weather was cold; it had been raining for two months, and no end was in sight. That was all I needed to hear. An Air National Guard KC-135 (DC-8) was leaving Nellis for Hickam, Hawaii, tomorrow, and the plane was empty.

I again sat in the cockpit with the crew. This crew was getting their monthly flight time, but every time I asked them to do an aileron roll, they thought I was crazy. What was wrong with these multi-engine pilots?

We arrived in Hawaii under partly cloudy skies and temperatures in the eighties. Someday, I thought, I would make this island my home. I checked into billeting for eleven dollars a night and then went swimming at the pool across the street. The next day, I took the number 19 bus to Ala Moana Beach Park for sixty cents and played tennis all day and then stopped off at CJ's in Restaurant Row and had a shellfish dinner before taking my sixty-cent bus ride back to Hickam.

It was February 18, President's Day, and there were no rooms available on base. So I took the number 19 and the number 51 bus to within a mile of NAS Barbers Point and then called a Can-Ride base shuttle, who brought me to the front door of the BOQ, where there were plenty of rooms because the base was so far away from Honolulu.

It was the end of February, and I'd had all the sun and fun I could take. Besides I was running out of money, so I caught a C-141 medivac flight from Hickam to Travis AFB. When we landed, I was greeted with cold, wet weather. I had trouble starting my Ranchero because (1) I'd left the battery cables connected and (2) moisture had gotten into the distributor cap due to the wet weather.

CHAPTER 9

CARIBBEAN

The mines in Nevada were busy in 1993, and I worked from April through mid-December, enabling me to put a few dollars away for my next trip. El Niño, a three hundred-mile-diameter mass of warm water, had arrived from the Southern Pacific, and the storms in the Sierras had already deposited five feet of snow. And it wasn't even winter yet. I left Reno on December 20 for Santa Rosa via Highway 70 through the Feather River Canyon because the highway was well maintained and snow chains weren't required—unlike Highway 80 over Donner Summit.

I had a pleasant Christmas and New Year's in Kenwood, California, with my mother, who was taking chemotherapy for a malignant tumor that had been removed five months earlier. It was getting cold, so I went to Travis and caught a C-5 to Dover AFB, Delaware, arriving in 65 degree clear weather. Because most flights from Dover went to Europe, I took another limo to Andrews.

The passenger terminal was crowded with reserves due to the Somalia incident. So, the first night, I managed to get a room in the enlisted quarters for eight dollars. Because there were no flights going south today, I went to the tennis courts and saw Jim Barnes and Alexander, who remembered me from last year. After spending the night off base at an Econo Lodge for forty-three dollars, I finally caught a C-9 medivac flight to NAS Norfolk, Virginia. And when we landed, the weather was overcast and raining. I checked into the BOQ for eight dollars and then had an excellent dinner at the Breezy Point O club and met some very friendly people.

The next morning, it was forty-five degrees and raining. After sharing a taxi with Jim Riseneck, a retired navy commander, we caught a C-22 (B-727) together to NAS Jacksonville, where it was cloudy and a pleasant seventy-three degrees.

The passenger terminal told me a flight was leaving for NAS Key West, Florida, from nearby NAS Cecil Field in a couple of days. So, I took a base shuttle to Cecil Field with Jim tagging along and checked into the BOQ. We watched the football playoffs that weekend. Buffalo beat Pittsburg, and San Francisco whipped Washington. Then I decided to get a haircut at the base barber shop, but even though I tried to tell the barber how I wanted it cut, he shaved me around the sides and left a clump of hair on the top. Guess I'd wear a hat for a while.

After walking to the golf course for breakfast the next morning, Jim and I caught a C-9 to Key West, with beautiful weather en route. We tried to check into the BOQ. But we were told us it was full, at which time Jim became very irate. He told the desk clerk he'd called ahead of time and had been told rooms were available, and he wanted to speak with the BOQ officer. Well, after the clerk made a few phone calls, he said to come back in a couple of hours, and he would see what he could do. We left our luggage there and walked down to the harbor and had conch soup and a couple of beers at the Half Shell Raw Bar. When we returned to the BOQ, two rooms were waiting for us. I guess you have to be a little forceful sometimes.

I went for a swim and some sun at the O club pool and then, that night, Jim and I went to town and had raw oysters and stone crab for dinner. The main street in Key West was more exciting than Bourbon Street in New Orleans because the people here were somewhat detached from the mainland. So, we had a great time that night watching girls dancing in the nude. We had breakfast the next morning at the Harbor

Lights and then decided to split up because Jim was heading back to San Diego, and I was going further south.

I caught a C-9 to Naval Station Roosevelt Roads, Puerto Rico, which means Rich Port in Spanish, flying over Nassau, Stella Maris Island, and the Bahamas. Roosy Roads was located on the northeast corner of Puerto Rico about fifty kilometers from downtown San Juan and was the largest US naval station, extending twenty-five square miles. I took a base shuttle from the terminal to the Bundy BOQ, located five miles away, and checked into a building that was built during World War II. Situated on top of a hill, it boasted coconut trees, manicured lawns, an eighteen-hole golf course, tennis courts, a fifty-meter swimming pool with fitness center, a movie theater, and an O club with fifty-cent beer—all overlooking the Caribbean Sea. What else did I need?

At night, you were serenaded by a small whistling frog called a coqui that sounded ten times its size. Gentle trade winds swept from the northeast and up to El Yunque, a rain forest that was three thousand feet above sea level and produced fifty inches of rain a year. The temperatures averaged between seventy and eighty-five degrees, with humidity around 80 percent. Every morning, the air was fresh and clean from the evening rain. When it got warm in the afternoon, the cool trades started to blow. And the sun shone 99 percent of the time.

That night I went to the O club and had fresh halibut at the captain's table with drinks and wine for only thirty dollars. The next day, I rented a car for thirty dollars and drove to Old San Juan, a clean part of town with shops selling items from around the world. I visited San Juan Cathedral, where the remains of Juan Ponce de Leon were buried, and then visited the San Jose Church, one of the most beautiful in the Americas. I stopped by Amadeus Restaurant for a beer and some arrowroot soup and then drove south via an expressway to the town of Ponce and visited the largest art museum on the island. I finished the day at the Roosy Roads O club, where I met Hector Morell, a very friendly and informative bartender who wanted me to meet his family in Ceiba, just outside the base.

The next day, I called base operations and found out a C-12 (Beechcraft King Air) was leaving for the Virgin Islands tomorrow and had an available seat. I met Captain Marcel Porret on the plane, who was the local veterinarian making his rounds, and he advised me to go to St. Croix because it was less crowded than the other islands. I got off at St. Croix and took a taxi to the town of Christiansted and checked into the Holger Denske Hotel for a whopping eighty dollars a night.

I walked around town and visited some historic sites including Fort Christiansvaern, where prisoners had been kept in dungeons in the early 1800s. I ate dinner at Tivoli's that night and had chicken and prosciutto and met some very friendly people. In fact, as you walked down the streets, everyone said good morning or good afternoon, an island custom.

The next day, I moved to the Danish Manor for sixty dollars, about the cheapest on the island because of the tourist season, although renting by the week would be cheaper. I went on Big Beards snorkeling tour to Buck Island for thirty dollars, including the diving equipment. It was a thirty-seven-foot catamaran that carried about twenty passengers and was captained by Mr. Simpson, a native of Antigua who was so black from the sun he was purple. We snorkeled around the reefs, relaxed in the sun, drank beer, and listened to island music. That night we all met at the Moonrakers, where Don Baggs, one of the crewmen, and I proceeded to sample every brand of rum they were serving.

I had breakfast the next morning at the Banana Club and then bought a T-shirt and took a ferry over to Cay Island to relax and recover from last night. I saw people parasailing off the back of a boat, so I thought, *What the hell?* I paid forty-five dollars and was winched out to three hundred feet above the water, where you could see the reefs, schools of fish, and turtles.

The next day, Don and his girlfriend invited me to spend the day with them at the West End Beach in Fredriksted, where we played volleyball, swam in the ocean, ate barbecued chicken, and drank a lot of beer. I saw in the paper that night that the Bills and Cowboys were going to the Super Bowl.

Well, I'd had enough fun here. And besides, it was too expensive. So, I took a Sunaire de Havilland twin otter for thirty-two dollars to the island of Vieques, just east of Puerto Rico. Some 80 percent of the island was owned by the US Navy, and when there are no maneuvers, numerous scalloped beaches were open to the public. I rented a Suzuki Samurai for fifty dollars and drove to Esperanza, a quiet little fishing village once the center of the sugar cane industry. I rented some snorkel equipment and swam two miles around a small island, observing undisturbed coral and fish that was not available on St. Croix due to the tourists.

I got a room at Banana's Hotel, had a few cocktails and a fresh grouper for dinner with wine, all for fifty dollars. I tell you, if you want to get away from it all, this island is the place. The price of a three-bedroom house in an exclusive area was under $100,000.

The next morning, I went snorkeling again and found a queen conch and fighting conch that I decided to take back with me to Puerto Rico. While I was returning the rental car, a guy about my age walked into the office. After some conversation, I found out he used to fly in the F-4 Phantom in Vietnam the same time I was there and was flying copilot for Virgin Airlines—what a small world.

I took a ferry for two dollars from Vieques to Fajarado Harbor on Puerto Rico. Halfway across the channel, the ferry came to a complete stop, and I thought we were going to be stranded. Then a US submarine leaped out of the water and crossed our bow at flank speed, creating a wake that almost threw everyone overboard.

After about two hours, we docked. I took a taxi for six dollars to the main gate at Roosy Roads and then the base shuttle to the BOQ. When I arrived, Ruthie, the girl at the front desk, remembered me. It was no problem getting a room, even though they were booked up; it's who you know, not what you know. I put the conch shells in my refrigerator and then went down to the Sea Breeze, an all-hands restaurant that served good food for a reasonable price. Then slept like a baby that night, with the trade winds blowing through my room.

I called Marcel at the vet clinic to tell him about my trip, and he gave me the name of a commissary officer, Anthony Carters, who was a tennis player. That night, I went to the O club and gave Hector the conch shells. He said he would fix me something the following night. The next morning, I met with Anthony, who beat me 6 to 2, 6 to 2 on the courts. I found out later he was the best player on the base; I'd get him.

I rented another car and drove to the Caribbean National Forest, the largest forest on Puerto Rico and the only tropical forest in the US National Forest system. It was usually referred to as El Yunque because of the peak, with over 100 billion gallons of annual rainfall and some 240 tree species. It was also home to fingernail-sized orchids, tree ferns, air plants, and such birds as the endangered Puerto Rican parrot. At the top of La Coca Falls, if one wants to risk the climb, are wild strawberries for the picking, which I managed to sample.

I arrived back at the base that night and went to the O club to find a conch salad that Hector had made waiting for me. Other people in the club thought the salad was on the menu and wanted the same order, but Hector tried to tell them I'd brought the shells from Vieques. So, the nice guy that I am, I shared it with them. I also gave Hector a coconut, and he proceeded to crack it open and make me a scotch and coconut juice drink.

An international exercise was taking place, and ships from all over the world were docked at Roosy Roads. Among them were Dutch, Portuguese, British, and Canadian frigates and cruisers. One night while all the officers were trying to impress each other at the O club, twenty-five Canadians stood up on the bar and dropped their pants. Needless to say, the base commander found out and told them, if they tried another stunt like that again, they would never be welcomed back to the base.

I called Marcel again and asked if he knew of any cars for sale. He hooked me up with the base food inspector, Bruce Richardson. Bruce had an old Honda Civic parked in back of the clinic that needed some work. It had blown a head gasket six months ago and hadn't run since. I told him that I'd tear down the engine if he'd help me reassemble it and split the cost fifty-fifty, and if it ran, I could use it for as long as I wanted. Well we towed the car to the base auto shop, which charged four dollars a day space, along with tools and supervision. I pulled the engine out and completely disassembled the motor, replacing the pistons, having the cylinder heads shaved, repairing the radiator, seating the valves, and installing new main bearings with Bruce's supervision. Eight days later, we had the engine back in the car, and when we turned the key, the damn thing started. My total cost, including labor, was only a hundred dollars. I didn't mind the hours I put into working on that car, as it was a learning experience; if I had to do it again, I could do it myself.

The first thing I did was to drive to the Navy Exchange to buy some snorkeling equipment. Then I headed for one of the beaches on the base and saw more fish and conch shells than I'd seen on Vieques because of the isolation.

I decided to stay on base for a few days just in case I'd forgotten to put everything back into that engine. One night, Hector invited me over to his house in Ceiba, which means "big tree" in Spanish, for a couple of beers and to meet his family. One of his cousins told me an apartment was for rent in town. So, we went over to take a look. It was a furnished one-bedroom with a kitchen and private bath for $250 a month. I thought, *What the hell? I'll take it.*

I checked out of the BOQ and then stopped off at the base thrifty store and bought pots, pans, cooking utensils, and silverware—all for fifty cents. You can't beat the military bases. Then I went to the commissary and stocked my apartment with a month worth of food for a hundred dollars, which would have cost twice as much in town.

I met Hiram Medina, the owner of the apartments. Hiram had a bar and pool table next to the apartments that was open Friday and Saturday nights. His brother-in-law would barbecue *pinchos*, a shish kebab made with pork. The popular beer in Puerto Rico, called Medalla, was made with rice instead of grain and was lighter in taste but wouldn't produce a headache if drank in excess, which we did.

One day, Hiram took me to see a house on two acres that overlooked the Caribbean. The asking price was just $40,000—what an investment. The only problem was I didn't have the money.

After repairing some minor bugs in the engine, I decided it was time to venture out. So, I bought a ticket on a ferry to Culebra, an island off the east coast of Puerto Rico. I borrowed a tent, sleeping bag, and ice chest from Hector's daughter and departed Fajardo Harbor for a two-hour ferry ride with my Honda on some choppy water to Culebra.

The island was used for target practice during World War II, and old tanks were still sitting on the beaches. I found Flamenco Beach, a secluded area with extremely white sand due to the deposit of coral. I pitched my tent in some shade trees near the beach with the sand and water as my front door, just like Robinson Crusoe. The ground was hard, so I used sand and leaves to make a soft bed and brought enough food and water to last me for three days, even though I could drive into a small town of Dewey if needed. I would dive for conch shells early in the morning while they were still on top of the sand because, when it got warmer, they would bury themselves.

One day, I met a couple from Brooklyn who'd been coming to this island for the past five years and thought it was the cleanest and quietest island in the Caribbean. Bathing attire was optional. But people wore something while I alone always ran around in the buff. I'd brought an underwater disposable camera with me and would take pictures of butterfly fish, parrot fish, squid, and stingrays. If I couldn't identify the fish, I had a plastic card with me that showed all the fish in the Caribbean.

One day while snorkeling about a mile off shore, I saw a school of small fish that they all suddenly disappeared. And then a six-foot barracuda went by me. I never swam so fast in my life, leaving a yellow stream behind because I pissed myself. When I reached the shore, I sat there for about an hour thinking about what could have happened if that barracuda had been hungry.

After my trek on the island, I went back to Dewey to catch the ferry back to Fajardo. While I was waiting, I had a pina colada at Marta's Restaurant at the wharf, where you could sit on a porch overlooking the Caribbean. When I arrived at Fajardo, I drove over to Hector's house and gave him some conch shells. Then I went to my apartment and gave the rest of the conches to Hiram and his family. That night, I played pool, ate pinchos, and drank Medalla with Hiram and his friends. Then I went to a fiesta in town because it was George Washington's birthday, and the Puerto Ricans looked for any excuse to party.

That weekend, I met Ruthie, my next-door neighbor, who worked at the base. We went out to a Mexican restaurant and then played pool and drank beer back at the apartments. She claimed to be a top pool player, but I taught her a few things about the game. I played tennis with Anthony the next day—6 to 2 and 6 to 4. That guy was tough, but one of these days.

On the way back to the apartments, I stopped off at a cock-fighting arena to watch an interesting sport. The cocks were trained for a year before their one and only fight, during which they wore spurs on their feet to cut the other bird. The cocks would fight until a bird either couldn't fight anymore or was killed, with most of the matches being won by luck with an eye or leg muscle cut. The cock-fighting arena was a folkloric spectacle, where people of all social backgrounds gathered together amid the clamor and confusion of the game, betting between $1 and $200 per fight.

The next day, I drove to the Ron Bacardi rum plant near San Juan for a tour. Bacardi originated in Cuba and was built in 1852, now producing fifty thousand gallons of rum per day. The process involved crushing the sugar cane and then boiling it to make molasses. Next, water and yeast were added to start the fermentation process, and the rum was stored in oak barrels to age for five years before bottling. After the tour, I went to an outside lounge at the plant, where you could sample several types of rum. The Bacardi 1873 was my favorite, but it wasn't for sale in America.

I bought a bottle and, with a pleasant glow, drove to the Hyatt Dorado Hotel and Golf Club, where I found Chi-Chi Rodriguez's house. But his head gardener said he was on tour and wouldn't be back for a few days. That afternoon, I drove to the south side of the island to the Plumas del Mar Resort and Tennis Club but was unable to pick up a tennis game. So, I headed back to Ceiba and had a few beers at the apartment with Ruthie.

The Honda was running well. So, today I planned to drive around the island, with my first stop being Albergue Olímpico, a training center for Olympic athletes from North America. I went to Camp Santiago Army Base and met Colonel Mike Koreda, the base commander, who put me up in the VIP quarters as his guest at no cost and then took me to a softball game between the base and a nearby town of Salinas.

The next morning, I drove west to Guanica, where I snorkeled at a beautiful coral beach and found a shell of a large sea urchin. Later that afternoon, I arrived in La Parguera, a popular resort town and found a paradores (guest hours) for twenty-five dollars and then went on a glass-bottom boat to Phosphorescent Bay, where millions of luminescent dinoflagellates lit up when you disturbed the water. I met a girl on the boat from Connecticut, but she couldn't stay in town because her girlfriend wanted to drive to Ponce that night—easy come, easy go.

The next day, I met with Tony Giannoni, a marine biologist who was a friend of Marcel Porret. Marcel was working on his PhD doing a study on a manatee he'd rescued a year and a half ago when it weighed 65 pounds. It now weighed 425 pounds and ate fifty pounds of vegetables a day. It was kept in a tank but would be released in a lagoon at Roosy Roads in a few weeks. I told Tony I was a geologist, and he suggested I check out the University of Puerto Rico's marine geology program to study the depletion of local coral. I said I'd think about it.

I headed further west to Boquerón, where stands of oysters, clams, and shark were along the beach being sold at very cheap prices. The island started turning north, where I arrived at Mayaguez a tuna-processing port with many historical sites, including a statue of Christopher Columbus.

While I was driving further north through the town of Aguadilla, the engine of my little Honda started losing power and finally quit. I took the air cleaner off and found water and oil in the carburetor, which came from a hose I'd forgotten to clean out. With the help of some Puerto Ricans and five dollars, I was on my way within an hour, heading to Punta Sardinera on the northwest coast of the island.

Punta Sardinera was a picturesque beach similar to the Oregon coast, the weather cold and windy and the surf high. I stayed in a beach cabin for twenty dollars and played pool that night with an American from Washington, a contractor who'd had been living here for twenty-five years. The only thing unpleasant about this place was the swarm of aggressive mosquitoes that attacked everything alive.

The next morning, I drove to Rio Camuy to see the limestone caves and underground rivers. But it rained so hard the tour was cancelled. As

I approached San Juan, I noticed that the Puerto Ricans would drive as fast as they could on the freeway, sometimes passing you on the right-hand shoulder. The speed limit signs were in miles per hour, but the distance signs were in kilometers, which made it difficult to tell how long it would take to get from one town to the next.

On my way through San Juan the Honda quit again; this time, it was an old transmission hose that Bruce had forgotten to replace. So, I rolled into a wrecking yard, and within an hour and ten dollars later, I was on my way again. If you were nice to these people, they will do anything to try and help you, as they were very self-conscious about Americans not liking them; I guess we think they're stupid and lazy.

As I traveled around the island, I noticed that Puerto Rico's agriculture was grown in the south. Crops included sugar cane, tomatoes, and pineapples, along with coffee, bananas, and mangos in the mountains. So far, I liked the west coast the best because it wasn't crowded, and the people were friendlier and more laid-back. And even though their income was low, they seemed to be happy with what they had.

I played pool with Ruthie at the apartments that night and told her about my trip around the island. She said the next time I should cross the middle of the island through the mountains, where I would meet the real Puerto Ricans. I was dancing with one of Hiram's friends that night, a black girl, and Hiram asked if Americans had any problems with interracial marriages. Because of the African slaves that were sent to Puerto Rico in the sixteenth century for the sugar cane plantations, interracial marriages here were very common. Just about everyone had some black blood in them.

I guess that Honda Civic was older than I thought because, the next morning, the transmission cable broke, and I could only go forward in second gear. On my way to the base, I heard a knocking sound coming from the engine. So, I parked it at the auto shop. I couldn't complain, though. I had driven that Civic for three weeks and had put 1,300 miles on it for about five cents a mile—not too bad. I told Bruce I'd help him replace the transmission cable if he loaned me a bicycle until I decided to leave Puerto Rico. I pedaled about fifteen miles a day from my apartment to the base playing tennis with Butch, snorkeling at the beach, and swimming at the base pool. What a life.

I heard that there was a shooting at Luquillo Beach south of San Juan between a Puerto Rican and an American at a deserted part of the beach—all over a stolen wallet.

Well, all good things must come to an end. It was March 1 and time to start heading back to Nevada. I gave the bike back to Bruce, who seemed happy about the Honda and said, if I ever came back and he still had the car, I was welcome to use it. Anthony invited me over to his house for fish gumbo that night after I finally beat him on the tennis court. He and his wife were African American but didn't show their color and took racial jokes very well.

The next day, Hiram drove me to the passenger terminal, where I caught a C-9 to Jacksonville with an admiral and his drug enforcement group, who were being relieved from a three-month duty in the Caribbean chasing drug runners. After arriving at NAS Jacksonville, I took an off-base shuttle from the hospital to NS Mayport, where a flight was scheduled for New Orleans in a few days. I had a steak dinner at the O club that night and then got drunk with some junior officers at the bar and talked about my hopping around on military flights for the winter.

I caught a T-39 Saberliner to NAS New Orleans, and because I used to fly in that same jet during training back in the '60s the crew let me sit up front during the flight. It was a reserve weekend at New Orleans, and the BOQ was full. So, I stayed off base at a Holiday Inn for fifty dollars; I sure missed those BOQ rooms for eight dollars. I rented a car from Enterprise for twenty-seven dollars and drove around town, playing tennis at a thirty-court tennis complex located in the city park.

That night, I checked into the Navy Lodge for thirty-five dollars and then went to the French Quarters and had crawdad brisque at Mulates before wandering around Bourbon Street, which didn't impress me. I hated to think what it must have looked like during Mardi Gras a few weeks ago.

I went to a chili cook-off the next day at the Naval Air Station for five dollars, and then I worked out at the base gym and later caught a

C-9 to NAS Corpus Christi, Texas. The BOQ was average, and the base personnel weren't very friendly. So, the next day, I rented a car from Enterprise for twenty-five dollars and drove to Brownsville to look at some property my mother had had trouble selling.

The plot map I had directed me to an area just north of Brownsville that had been developed ten years ago. Unfortunately, the map was wrong. The actual property was located in an undeveloped area that was still pastureland and not approved for development.

I drove down to Matamoros across the border in Mexico and got a haircut for five dollars, dinner for five dollars, and an iguana belt for twenty-four dollars. I drove back to NAS Kingsville and checked into a beautiful suite for eight dollars. I went for a swim that night at the Texas A&M University's indoor fifty-meter pool and, later, had dinner at the base bowling alley because the O club was closed.

I spent the next day at Port Arkansas on Padre Island, just three days before spring break, when 250,000 students were expected to arrive. I stopped at a deli and had twenty-two oysters for five dollars and then went to the beach for a little fun and sun. That night, I ate at Fat Daddy's and ordered "Dump on the Table"—which consisted of shrimp, crawfish, sausage, and potatoes that were brought out in a bucket and actually dumped on a paper tablecloth on your table. When you were finished, the waiters would gather up the tablecloth and throw it away. Who needs a dishwasher?

Because there were no flights going west from either Kingsville or Corpus Christi, I returned the rental car and then took an off-base shuttle from the base hospital at Corpus Christi to Kelly AFB. At the passenger terminal, I met Michelle, an ROTC cadet also going west. After the flight was cancelled, we checked into the BOQ and had a two-for-the-price-of-one dinner at the O club. It rained all night due to a storm coming down from Alaska, and when I got up the next morning it was fifty degrees outside. We caught a C-5 to Travis, where the weather was clear and seventy degrees. But apparently, a lot of snow had fallen in the Sierra Nevada mountains, so I guess Reno's eight-year drought was over. My car started right up, as I had disconnected the battery cables before I left and cleaned the moisture out of the rotor.

CHAPTER 10

VENEZUELA

The summer was not a good time for my mother. Her health deteriorated, with cancer spreading to her lungs. And she finally passed away in June 1994. I worked all year, including a cold winter in Elko sitting outside on a drill rig in three feet of snow. I was either crazy or else I needed the money. I left Santa Fe Pacific Gold in January 1995 and spent the rest of the winter and spring flying back and forth to Hawaii on MAC aircraft. Spring was so cold in Reno that I didn't return until the middle of June. Then I played tennis until the middle of September when I went to work for Viceroy Gold in Searchlight, south of Las Vegas, for a couple of months. It was a very relaxing job, cutting and logging core samples and playing tennis after work with the mine manager at the company's ranch, which had been purchased from movie magnates Rex Bell and Clara Bow. I even had the opportunity to watch the '95 Davis Cup at Caesar's Palace in Las Vegas, observing Pete Sampras, Andre Agassi, and Todd Martin defeat the Swedish team.

After that job in Searchlight, I returned to Reno and then drove down to Travis AFB on November 21. There, I ran into Kurt Tang, a retired air force major friend of mine in the PX parking lot. We played tennis on base and I beat him 6 to 0 and 6 to 0 and felt so sorry for him that I took him to dinner at the O club that night. I met Trish the bartender, who showed me her tan line behind the bar, and Kurt just sat there with his mouth open.

The next day, I parked my car in the long-term parking for five dollars a week and caught a C-17 Globemaster to Charleston AFB, South Carolina, via NAS North Island, where they dropped off some Navy SEALs and their boat coming back from Egypt. The C-17 was a nice new aircraft, fast and quiet, that would eventually replace the C-130 for short-field takeoff and landing. On the flight, I met Frank Olcott, a retired army colonel from Ft. Lauderdale. We shared a two-for-one steak dinner at the O club.

It was Thanksgiving Day, and everything on base was closed except the golf course, where I walked to get breakfast. At one o'clock that afternoon, I went to the O club and had a fantastic turkey dinner and great conversation with Frank and Juan, a retired major from San Juan. Frank said he was traveling around to all the sixty-five Chart House Restaurant, and when he was done eating at them, he would get two free airline tickets around the world.

The following day, Frank and I caught a C-141 to MacDill AFB, Tampa Bay, Florida, where we rented a car for thirty-seven dollars and then drove to Jacksonville to pick up Frank's car. After turning in the rental, we drove to Ft. Lauderdale, arriving at nine o'clock that night, just in time to go to the bars and meet all of Frank's pals. He was seventy years old but still liked the young dollies, as he called them. Frank put me up in his apartment for three days so I could go to the beach every day and drink with Frank at the bars every night—what a life.

On November 28, Frank drove me to the Miami International Airport, where I had bought a round-trip ticket to Caracas, Venezuela, on American Airlines for $300. That included two Crown Royals, a steak dinner, three small bottles of red wine, and a couple more to take with me after the flight.

The Caracas Airport was on the coast, and it took forty-five minutes by taxi to get to the city, where I found the Hotel Coliseo for thirty dollars a night. The city had 5 million people, too many cars, and was too dangerous to walk around in at night. The weather was perfect, though, with temperatures around eighty degrees during the day and cool nights because the city was a thousand feet above sea level. The money exchange rate was 300 bolívares to 1 US dollar, and that varied by 50 bolívares because of the unstable government.

I met Igor Pankovs, a geologist originally from Latvia, who told me to go to Cuidad Bolívar to look for gold or diamonds. I rode a bus south to Bolívar via Puerto La Cruz for six dollars. The seven-hour ride crossed the Orinoco River, the seventh largest in the world. For six dollars, I checked into the Hotel Italia, with a balcony that overlooked the river. Then I met Ricki from British Guyana, who spoke better English then I did. We went to the Caroni River, where companies, including some from the United States, owned hydraulic missile dredges, extracting gold and diamonds thirty feet below the surface. A lot of rigs were for sale for $15,000, with a net monthly profit of $10,000. But you had to stay on board twenty-four hours a day, and it was very dangerous. When I got back to town, I bought a forty-nine-point (half-carat) uncut diamond from a dealer for a hundred dollars, planning to have it cut when I get back to the United States.

Due to the corruption in the election poles, there was uneasiness in the city. In fact, while I was walking downtown, a shooting broke out, and I had to drop to the ground so I wouldn't get hit by any stray bullets. Finally, a unit of paratroopers landed to try and control the shooting spree.

When I got back to the hotel, I met Gilbert, a sixty-two-year-old engineer from Texas who had come down here twenty years ago to strike it rich extracting gold. He'd accumulated over $750,000. But the other miners had eventually stolen everything he had, and he was now destitute and waiting tables in cheap hotels just to put food in his mouth.

I bought a ticket on VIASA Air to Sao Paulo, Brazil, for $975 and asked the travel agent if I needed a visa. She said my passport would suffice. I spent the day at the Sheraton Hotel in Macatu near the Caracas Airport playing tennis and swimming, all for ten dollars. Then I boarded a DC-10 for a six-hour flight, including a great dinner and all the wine I wanted to drink. When I got off the plane in Sao Paulo, customs told me I needed a visa and put me back on the plane to Caracas. Well, that was a long flight back to Caracas because there was nothing I could do about the visa.

When I landed, I tried arguing with the travel agent and the airlines, but they said it was my responsibility to check with international laws; such is life. I checked back into the Hotel Coliseo and met the owner's daughter and told her of my plight. She gave me an unlimited pass to Centro Italo Venezolano, a sports club with eight outside clay tennis courts; four swimming pools, including a seventy-meter lap pool; and restaurants and shops. Everything eventually works out. The club was partly owned by Italians, as were the hotels and restaurants because 20 percent of the population here was Italian. Well, I spent the next week at my own private club playing tennis, swimming, and working on my tan in my skimpy Venezuelan bathing suit.

The city of Caracas sat in a valley with mountains up to two thousand meters (six thousand feet). One day, I went for a hike to Las Adjuntas, a waterfall in El Avila National Park that produces sweet, unpolluted water, I thought.

I had dinner at my hotel that night with Adriana, who worked for a glass company in Colombia and was here selling some very unusual pieces. The Colombians were very light-skinned due to their Spanish and German heritage. One day, for about twenty cents, I rode all over town on the Metro system checking out certain parts of the city and found a *Daily Journal*, an American newspaper that came out three times a week, to find out what was going on in the United States. The best places to eat in town were Italian restaurants specializing in lasagna. For twelve dollars with wine, you get impeccable service, especially if they knew you were and American.

I decided to head south again. I took a taxi to the Caracas Airport and managed to get the last airplane ticket to Puerto Ayacucho at the beginning of the Amazon jungle only four degrees north of the equator. After we landed, I joined Camturama Tour for a couple of days to experience the natives in the jungle called Yanomami. The people were small because of the lack of calcium in their diet. The natives as young as five years old had their noses and mouths pierced with bones and had their hair cut in a pageboy fashion.

We cruised down the Orinoco River, which separated Venezuela from Colombia, a drug-stricken country that had drug rehab centers along the riverbanks. This kept the recovering addicts, as young as ten, from escaping due to the size of the river and its strong current. The river has piranhas, dolphins, and a barracuda-like fish with two front teeth so long that they went through two holes in the creature's head when its mouth was closed.

After the tour, I went to Ayacucho and checked into the Amazonas Hotel, which offered a restaurant, bar, and pool, for nine dollars a day. The humidity was almost unbearable, my skin was starting to shred, mosquitoes were eating me alive, and you couldn't use the room's air conditioner because you'd catch a cold. I met Juan Carlos, who took me across the river by ferry to Cazaurito, a small town in Colombia that only required a passport to enter.

The people were prettier and happier than the Venezuelans, and I immediately met a thirty-year-old girl who wanted to come back to the United States with me. It was the Christmas holiday, and people were in a very festive mood. So I took Milaidyz, my hotel room maid, out for dinner. After a couple of hours, she said she loved me and also wanted to come back to the United States.

Well, the Europeans were starting to arrive, so I guessed it was time to get out of this infested jungle country. I managed to get the last airline ticket again back to Caracas, and while I was waiting at the airport, I saw an old high-wing aircraft that made the first flight over Angel Falls (3,200 feet) in 1927.

When I got to Caracas, I checked into the Continental Hotel for twenty-three dollars. The hotel had a balcony with a view of Mount El Avila and the Humboldt Hotel on top, which hadn't been open for thirty years. I played tennis and swam at my private club for a few days. Then on New Year's Day, I hiked up to the Humboldt Hotel, a five-hours journey that gave me a view of the Caribbean Sea on one side and the Atlantic Ocean on the other. That night, people fired off explosives in town to celebrate the New Year that sounded like dynamite. I guessed you could buy anything in town for a price. In fact, one night, I had the bellboy bring a twenty-year-old Venezuelan girl to my room for sixty dollars who would do anything I asked of her.

On January 5, 1996, I bought a ticket for thirty dollars on Avensa to Merida at the beginning of the Los Andes Mountains. It was a beautiful and clean city about 4,500 feet in elevation, with narrow cobblestone streets and quaint European-style houses. The climate was the exact opposite of Ayacucho, with warm, dry days and cool nights and no mosquitoes, thank god. For thirteen dollars a day, I stayed at the Hotel Teleferico, which offered a cable television with some American channels. Next to the hotel was the longest and highest aerial tram in the world. It took you through three stations, going from five thousand feet to fifteen thousand feet. Unfortunately, it had been shut down for two years because the cable on the last station broke, and two people were killed.

Well, I managed to make the right contacts and caught a ride up with the workers to the third station. From there, I hiked to the summit and met some natives hauling vegetables, grain, and medicine by mules from a valley on the other side of the mountain. On the way back down that afternoon, I had to ride in the cargo cart, which barely had enough room for seven people and supplies and left me literally hanging onto the side with nothing but thousands of feet between me and the ground below.

The next day, I took a bus to the town of Taby and hiked for six hours to the Coromoto lagoon at nine thousand feet to see crystal clear water coming down the mountain from the glaciers above. What a magnificent country.

I checked Merida out and found some hard-surface tennis courts with good players and also an Olympic size swimming pool at the university. The food here was excellent and cheap. For example, a complete breakfast cost only two dollars, or a fresh trout dinner was only four dollars. What a deal. The town was laid out like New York City, with numbered streets in one direction and numbered avenues in another, so it was easy to find a corner.

I stayed for two weeks, playing tennis, swimming, hiking, relaxing in mineral hot springs, riding the minibus for twenty cents, getting a haircut for $1.40, and eating great food. One night at a hotel restaurant, a guy wanted to exchange a $100 bill for bolívares and would take 250 when the rate was 350. So, I thought, *What the hell? I'll make a quick buck.*

I left Merida on January 18 on a bus to El Vigia and sat with Nidya, a seventeen-year-old girl, who helped me get to the airport. We had breakfast together in the terminal and talked about Venezuela verses the United States. The young girls here were a lot more mature than their counterparts in the United States. I flew to Valencia, the third largest city, via San Antonio and Maracaibo and then took a bus to Chichiriviche, a fishing village on the Caribbean coast three hundred kilometers west of Caracas.

I met Manual Moreano, a Colombian who owned the Vera Cruz Restaurant. He found me a nice hotel called Primera for thirteen dollars a night. I took a boat tour out to some limestone caves located in small islands and met a Brazilian girl touring with her family in another boat. We spent the day together.

That night, I got drunk at Manual's bar and ate some tainted shellfish. In my room that night, I got sick and was up all night with diarrhea and vomiting. When I woke up, I was extremely weak. Manual said I probably got a parasite and should head back to the United States and get some medical attention, or I might die here.

It rained hard for the next few days. Between the diarrhea, the mosquitoes, and the loss of twenty pounds, I thought it was time to get the hell out of here. I took an agonizing six-hour bus ride to Caracas and then flew back to Miami and eventually started feeling better, I thought. I flew down to NAS Key West and was picked up by the naval air station duty driver and taken to the Trumbo BOQ. It sure felt good to get back to the States and eat food I recognized.

I relaxed for a few days on the base, playing tennis and swimming, but I was still a little weak from that parasite, or whatever it was. I had dinner at Captain Jack's in town, and when I attempted to pay with that $100 bill I'd gotten in Merida, I was told it was a fake; the acid mark the pen made was brown instead of black under ultraviolet light. I played dumb and said I'd gotten it from the bank and would take it back.

I tried to get a flight to Roosevelt Roads, but no planes were scheduled. So I caught a C-9 to Norfolk and landed in a cold, wet storm. But at least it wasn't as bad as the snowstorm that had just hit Reno. I met a retired army major who was a stock trader. He talked me into buying Midisoft, which might be bought out by Microsoft one day. I bought two thousand shares at two and a quarter. I watched the Cowboys beat the Steelers on a big screen at the BOQ. Then the next day, I caught a C-141 to Hickam but had to spend the night at McChord, Washington, where it was snowing, with temperatures in the twenties. It was sure hard to get used to all these temperature changes.

The next morning, after replacing a starter valve on the number four engine of the C-141, we departed for Hickam, arriving at four o'clock in the afternoon. That night, a wild lightning storm hit Oahu and dropped three inches of rain in an hour, but at lease it was warm.

I woke the next morning the end of January to a picture-perfect day. So I took the number 19 bus to Diamond Head Tennis Center (DHTC) and saw all my friends from Canada. After tennis, I walked to the beach for a swim and some sun and then went to a 7-Eleven and bought a monthly bus pass for twenty-five dollars and finally got rid of that $100 bill— what a relief.

The next day while playing tennis, I got hit in the left eye with a ball by a local named Martin Henson, who to this day has never said he was sorry; what an asshole. I went to Triple Army Hospital and found out the pupil had been damaged and was permanently dilated so I had to wear sunglasses during the day. It could have been worse. Seven years ago, Doris Hackman, a ranked senior player, got hit and lost the sight in her eye but still plays and wins too.

I went apartment hunting and found a studio apartment at 2551 Kapiolani Boulevard for $540 a month; it included a refrigerator, sheets, and a shared kitchen. There was a supermarket nearby, plus restaurants, and it was only thirty minutes to the tennis courts.

I was trying to get accustomed to Hawaiian food at a restaurant that served laulau (pork in taro leaves) and poi made from the taro root and some items I couldn't even pronounce. I filled my refrigerator with groceries that cost 30 percent more than on the mainland but were still cheaper than eating out every night.

I have trouble seeing the ball in the bright sunlight, so I bought a pair of dark Oakley sunglasses, and at night I saw a rainbow of colors around streetlights.

Jim, the manager at the apartments, sold me a thirteen-inch black-and-white television for forty dollars so I could catch up on the news. The Pro Bowl game was this weekend, with all the top football players, including Jerry Rice, walking around their hotels flaunting all their money.

One day after getting beat on the tennis court by a local wearing beach thongs, I hiked to the top of Diamond Head crater and took pictures of Waikiki, Kapiolani Park, and the tennis courts. I met Brad Chuck and Ellie Montana, who run the DHTC and maintain the courts and surroundings. Both were retired military and had been living here for twenty years. I met Ray Yaurcheck at the tennis courts. He had an old bicycle he let me use, so now it only took me fifteen minutes to get to the courts, and I had a little more freedom to venture out. I'd get up at six o'clock in the morning and have a bowl of cereal, bike to the corner for a newspaper, arrive at DHTC at seven thirty, play tennis until eleven o'clock, bike to Diamond Head Beach for a swim and some sun, and then pedal around town checking out the area. I'd be back to my apartment by cocktail hour and then head out to a restaurant for a hot meal, finally returning home to watch a little television before I hit the sack.

One day, I rode downtown for a five-dollar haircut at the barber college and found Chinatown, where fruit and vegetables were very inexpensive.

The island did strange things to tourists. For instance, a man brought his wife on a business trip from Cincinnati, and within a couple of days, she disappeared. Apparently, she was living with the homeless and, one night, was seen running naked on the beach but disappeared again. Her husband tried but failed to locate her. So, he went back home to his family and waited. Eventually, he received a letter from her, stating that, because she'd been brought up in a small conservative town, had married and had children at a young age, and had never left Cincinnati, she was trying to find herself and would be home when she did.

Sometimes, I played at the Kapiolani Courts because the group was comprised of locals and was friendlier, unlike the tourists at DHTC. I met Chris Ly, a Chinese woman born in Vietnam who had a lot in common with me when it came to tennis, swimming, and eating out. But it seemed she was looking for a husband.

I was still weak from that ordeal in Venezuela, so I went to a Chinese herbalist, who gave me Sai Si tea for the poison, Dongshong Chou to cleanse me out, reishi for the gas, and some pills similar to ginseng to increase my energy level. Well, it worked while you were taking the medicine, but when you stopped, the symptoms returned.

Kilauea was erupting on the big island of Hawaii, so I bought a round-trip ticket to Hilo on Aloha Airlines for a hundred dollars that included a rental car. I arrived in a rainstorm and then drove to the volcano. While I only saw minimal activity, the volcano has added five miles to the island since its eruption.

I went to Punalu'u Beach, with its black sand, where the weather had cleared up, and saw a green sea turtle (*honu*) that would come up on the beach every day and get fed by the tourists. He had to be at least seventy-five years old. I put the top down on my LeBaron and drove to Kailua Kona on the west side of the island, which was more populated because of the weather. Hilo was the cheapest place to live on the island right now, but I predicted, within ten years, that would all change, and now would be a good time to buy either a house or some property.

As I drove back to Hilo that afternoon, it started raining. But I left the top down anyway. We flew back to Honolulu via Maui in and out of the rain, as a storm was coming up from the Marshall Islands and moving through the area, creating waves at Waikiki Beach as high as ten feet that were washing up onto the streets. There were two weather patterns in Hawaii. The trade winds came out of the northeast in the winter and brought rain to the Koolau mountains, sending cool breezes over the island and surf on the North Shore as high as thirty feet. In the summer, the Kona winds came out of the south, sending warm, wet humid weather over the island and high surf to the south shores like Waikiki.

I biked to the Ala Wai Yacht Harbor one day and found boats selling for $300 a foot that you could live on in the harbor for $180 a month; it sounded interesting. I biked to the Ala Moana Tennis Center but it was hard to get a game until the locals got to know your level of play. So, I kept going back until someone finally asked me to join them. The level of play was higher than that at both DHTC and Kapiolani. So, maybe playing here would improve my game. Across the street from the courts was Ala Moana Beach Park, where the locals hung out and you could swim a two-kilometer lap and be protected by a reef so the waves didn't toss you around. Most locals had the same routine around here because the island was small. After a while, there was nothing else to do. So, I wasn't sure this was the place to retire.

It was the end of February, and the tourists were starting to leave the island; it was getting a little quieter, which I liked. Maybe I'd stay here until March—or at least until the temperature in Reno reached seventy degrees—because I wasn't spending a lot of money living here.

One night, Chris and I were playing tennis at Kapiolani Park while listening to Willie Nelson and Leon Russell at the nearby Waikiki Shell Outdoor Theater—only in Hawaii. Later, we walked to the Royal Hawaiian for a couple of mai tais and then went to the Dynasty near the Hilton Hawaiian Village for a great Chinese dinner that she ordered. She owned a furnished condo and was always trying to rent it to me for $900 a month. But I was happy where I was.

My how the time flies; it was the end of March already, and the temperature in Reno was seventy-four degrees. A flight was leaving Hickam for Travis on the twenty-seventh. Plus, it was spring break, and military families would be going back to the mainland and filling up the planes. I took the bike to the Elks Club parking lot and chained it to a tree for Ray, checked out of my apartment, and then took the numbers 3 and 19 to Hickam AFB. I caught a KC-10 that night to Travis AFB. I went up into the cockpit and had a spectacular view of a comet near the big dipper that had a tail extending halfway across the sky.

I arrived at Travis the next morning, so I checked into the BOQ and slept half the day. Then I went to the O club and saw Trish and showed her my pictures of Venezuela before going behind the bar to show her my tan line. She proceeded to show me her tan, along with a white heart she's blocked out on her cheek, and I don't mean the cheek on her face.

I drove back to Reno the next morning. And would you believe I hit a snowstorm going over Donner Summit? To make things worse, the temperature in Reno had dropped to thirty-eight degrees. I guess that seventy-four degrees had just been a teaser to get me to come home. I Met Tilly and Jo, Al and Dolly, and Betty at Johnny's Little Italy Restaurant that night without anyone knowing I was back. What a welcoming.

CHAPTER 11

LIGHTNING RIDGE, AUSTRALIA

I did some exploration work in Nevada on and off during the summer, and while I was in Reno, I would have breakfast every morning with Tilly, Frank Margrave, and a bunch of other millionaires. All they talked about was loaning out money on first deeds of trust. Any loans too small for them they would let me have. Thanks to Tilly, my loans were increasing and I was starting to live off the interest I made every month. I told the guys I was thinking of going back to Australia, and Frank, who was a Nevada miner, wanted me to find some black opals for him.

I left Reno November 12, 1996, in my trusty Ranchero for Travis and then caught a C-20 (Gulfstream V) and was in Hickam, Hawaii, by five o'clock that evening—all for $2.75, the cost of a box lunch. Hickam BOQ was full, so I checked into Naval Station Pearl Harbor BOQ for fifteen dollars with a guaranteed room for three nights. I took the bus to the Australian consulate in Honolulu to get a visa and then went to the DHTC to play tennis with the crowd after rolling the courts because of the rain.

I saw Doris Hackman, who was teaching at the Pearl Harbor Tennis Complex. I told her my tennis must be getting better because I'd played five sets and hadn't lost yet. She said, "Just wait. You will."

It had been raining so much this winter that the island was saturated, and mud was sliding everywhere. Slick Willy and Hilary Clinton arrived here en route to the Philippines and gave Governor Cayetano $1,000,000 for disaster relief from the rain.

I met Gordon Handley, a ranked senior player whose son, Steve, ran an opal mine at Lightning Ridge, Australia, and said to look him up when I get there. I saw Sam Uta, a Tongan from the Kapiolani courts who was a bartender at the Mai Tai Bar in the Royal Hawaiian Hotel and always served me three strong mai tais for the price of one; I hoped he never got caught. I had lasagna at Tratotias next to the Sheridan Hotel in Waikiki, but it didn't compare with the lasagna I'd had in Venezuela.

The trade winds started blowing, which cleared out the rain. So, I went to the Ala Moana Courts to get some better games. It seemed there were three categories of tennis. At DHTC, where tourists came, weren't sure what kind of game you'd get into. At Kapiolani Park, older locals—both haole (the white man) and Hawaiians played—but you had to leave the court after each set. Ala Moana was where the hard-core players hung out, among them Duley Kam, who was a nationally ranked player in the '70s.

I'd been swimming at Ala Moana Beach Park, starting at five hundred meters, and I was up to one kilometer three times a week.

I was having trouble getting a seat out of Hickam to Australia, so I bought a ticket at SATO, a military travel agency, and reserved a flight on December 3 to Sydney on Air New Zealand for $450 one way.

Every Friday night, I walked from the BOQ at Pearl Harbor one and a half miles through beautiful Aina Park along the waterfront of the harbor to the Hickam Officer Club. During happy hour, you could eat all you wanted (prime rib, fish, salad, and the like) just for buying a beer. I thought I'd found a gold mine.

One day I went to Diamond Head Beach for a swim and saw young men sitting around waiting for rich old widows to come down from their condos. It seemed as though they were looking for each other. I supposed it was part of life.

I checked out of the BOQ and then took a bus to the airport to store my luggage before heading to Ala Moana to play tennis for the day. After a shower at the beach and dinner at the Yum Yum Tree in Ward Center, I took the bus back to the airport and departed at two o'clock in the morning on December 3 on a B-747-200 for a six-hour flight to Nadi, Fiji.

The weather there was mild, with very friendly people who spoke their own native Fijian language. After an hour layover, we departed for a two-hour flight to Auckland, New Zealand. The weather there was mild, with the temperature in the seventies, and everything was very green because of the high rainfall. After a couple of hours, we departed Auckland for a two-our flight to Sydney, arriving at five o'clock in the afternoon.

I took a bus to the Barnsley Hotel in Kings Cross, an area similar to Greenwich Village in New York. I got a room for A$40 (US$24) that had a double bed, a sink, and a closet but shared community bathrooms and showers. I walked down to the Sauna Pub and had a Guinness stout with 6 percent alcohol, not the 3.8 percent you got in the United States. You just had to drink a little slower.

I went to Eden Travel later and bought a ticket to Lightning Ridge for A$200; the flight left in a couple of days. Then I went to the Fountain Restaurant and had a lasagna dinner with wine for A$12. The next morning, I woke up and saw full-figured women on my floor walking around wearing bath towels. I found out later they tried to keep male and female guests on separate floors, but that was the only room left—rough life.

I talked with owners, Charles and Stella, about looking for opals, and they sold me a bottle of rough stones for A$40 so I could get used to the colors before I got to Lightning Ridge. I swam at the Boy Charlton Pool near Sydney Park and then found Rushcutters Bay Tennis Club and met Leslie Turner, who played in the quarter finals at the French Open in the '60s, and hit with me on clay courts.

The next morning, I took a one-hour flight to Dubbo, New South Wales, in a Saab 340 turboprop, followed by a very nervous one-hour flight to Lightning Ridge in a Cessna 310 through a thunderstorm with a pilot who still had pimples on his face. After we landed, I told him about my navy flying experience in Vietnam, and he said he was glad I hadn't mention that before, or he would have been too nervous to fly with me.

The terminal at Lightning Ridge consisted of a covered bench with a telephone. I guessed I was in the outback now. Fortunately. there was another passenger on the flight who was an opal miner and gave me a ride to town about five kilometers away. I checked into the Wallangulla Motel for forty-five dollars, a price that included breakfast. Then I walked across the street to the Lightning Ridge Bowling Club (LRBC) for a beer. Within thirty minutes, I'd met half a dozen old miners, including Gus Knee who had been here thirty-five years and invited me to come out to his mine the next day.

The town was very unique because it got its name from a lightning storm that killed six hundred sheep, a shepherd, and his dog in the late 1800s. It had grown from two hundred residents thirty-five years ago to about two thousand today, with another six thousand or so living on claims in the opal fields. It was the only black opal deposit in the world that came in different varieties, black- and gray-based solids, doublets, triplets, mosaics, crystals, and boulders, all ranging from blues (the easiest to find) to reds (the most sought after).

Opal is a silicate that is weathered from the overlying rocks that percolate over thousands of years through a sandstone to a clay stone below. It's usually found at a depth of about forty feet but because of faulting. Some opals have been seen on the surface, and that was how they were first discovered in the early 1900s. Mining opals begins with a claim that is surveyed (fifty meters by fifty meters) and then registered, two claims per person, at a cost of A$80 per claim plus a A$100 refundable bond. Next, a nine-inch drill is used to find sandstone levels and possible color at a cost of A$100 per hole. If it looks promising, a three-foot diameter bucket drill with a reamer is sunk to about forty feet; ladders are dropped into the hole, and a two-man crew descends with jackhammers to follow the clay stone level. A seven-foot ceiling is made so it's easy to maneuver with electric lighting and a ten-inch PVC pipe connected to a blower above to extract the mined dirt that's loaded in a dump truck and transported to an agitator for washing.

These agitators are converted cement mixers that run in reverse, with screens on the sides for the clay to wash out.

After a couple of days, the washed rock is tailed out and nodules (nobbies) are sorted out, both with and without color. The nobbies are then rubbed down with a grinding wheel to determine color, shape, and value. The final process is to cut and polish the stones to a maximum carat weight, usually in an oval shape, with the entire process taking less than a week, depending on operating breakdowns.

An individual should expect to spend A$50,000 for equipment without any guarantee of return. So a lot of miners go into partnership with drillers, diggers, agitator owners, and claim owners, splitting the profits. Opal buyers come from all over the world especially Asia and set up in the motel rooms in town to buy opals in the rough, rubbed or finished. Depending on the quality, stones varied from A$50 a carat to A$10,000 a carat due to the pattern and display and clarity of colors.

The Australians were very hospitable. Even if they were down on their luck, they'd invite you in for tea (dinner) and stretch two plates of food intended for just the two of them into three. Honesty was the best policy in town because there was a lot of trust in the opal business. If you cheated someone mining or cutting opal, you'd be blackmarked, defriended, and never trusted again.

I joined the LRBC, and the first Sunday morning, I was introduced to the art of lawn bowling, a game that allotted each player one small white ball and four larger black balls. The idea was to get as close to the white ball as you could, bowling alternately with the other person. The only problem was that the black balls were not round and had a slight curve, depending on which side you were holding the ball. If you forget and the ball curved the wrong way and went into another team's game, you had to buy a round of beer for everyone—sometimes as many as twenty people; and of course you know who had to buy a couple of rounds.

I also went golfing one day, and the only green grass was a small patch at each driving tee. Then it was out in the dirt rough with rocks, brush, fallen tree branches, and gullies and, of course, kangaroos and snakes. When you got to the hole, it was surrounded by oiled sand that you raked smooth from the hole to your ball before you putted.

I also found some tennis courts behind the LRBC that consisted of sandy outdoor carpet. But it was too hot this time of year, and nobody was playing. Another pastime was the pistol club, which most miners—including Gus's wife, Michele—belonged to. She had run away from home in Sydney a couple of years ago on her motorcycle and had wound up in Lightning Ridge, where she'd met Gus. They'd gotten married, even though he was sixty-five, and she was only twenty-six, the same age as Gus's son. Gus owned a bucket drill rig, and the two of them drilled together for other miners, receiving a share of the opal finds for their efforts.

Lamb was the cheapest way to put food on the table. So, one day, Gus and I drove out to his friend's sheep ranch, and I bought a whole butchered lamb for only A$30 and put it in Gus's freezer.

I met Michael Smith, a recovered alcoholic, who was one of the top ten black opal cutters in the world. We hit it off because he liked to fly and enjoyed listening to my war stories. I spent the next three months cutting opals under his supervision and polishing over three hundred stones that I'd either bought from miners or that Jim had lying around his shop.

Since my motel bill was running up, I decided to share a flat for A$70 a week with a bloke I met at the LRBC. Unfortunately, all he was interested in was having me invest in his gold and opal schemes. Jim lived four miles out of town, so Michele found me a 1987 Yamaha AG 200 motorcycle for A$300 that needed a little work. After a month, my roommate finally got on my nerves. So, I found a twenty-one-foot Viscount Caravan with a canvass annex for US$1,700. I moved into a caravan park for A$40 per week. Now all I needed was citizenship and I was here permanently?

It was the Christmas holiday season. And all Gus, Michele, and I did was visit different houses of his mates every afternoon for drinks and a barbie (barbeque). Aussies ate like the English, with breakfast about nine or ten o'clock in the morning, lunch around two o'clock in the afternoon, and dinner between eight and nine o'clock in the evening.

I was having trouble with directions down here because the sun moved north as the days got shorter, the opposite of North America. So, I'd look toward what I thought was north, and it was south. And yes, the magnetic current caused water to move clockwise going down the drain.

The sheilas (women) here were beautiful and very easygoing. But I didn't think I'd meet one in Lightning Ridge because the ratio was eight men to one woman, mainly due to the harsh conditions in the outback.

You couldn't always trust everyone, especially "ratters," a group of ex-miners who sat in the Diggers Rest Bar across the street from the Black Opal Motel and saw who was selling opals. Later that night, they'd go out to the seller's claim and mine out what was left of his findings. They'd use night goggles and sophisticated communications equipment, making them very difficult to apprehend. A few get caught though and were tarred and feathered and hung from a tree for a few days. Some were tossed down a mining hole, which was filled in, and were never heard from again. It was like the old West, with some miners packing pistols and the local police seeming to look the other way and letting them take care of their own—food for thought.

It was the middle of January 1997, and the temperature averaged 45 degrees Celsius (above 110 degrees Fahrenheit). But underground was a constant 22 degrees Celsius (72 degrees Fahrenheit). In fact, there was an opal town in the outback that built their houses partly underground.

I decided to take out two claims in an area called T Bone II, about forty kilometers west of town where other miners were getting some color. I had Wally the Swede drill a couple nine-inch holes but couldn't find any good sandstone levels. So, I gave the claims back to the mining association, all for a total cost of A$450.

Jim Middleton's son Garth said there were a couple of promising claims at Granny's Flat next to T Bone II. So, maybe I'd give it another try when I returned to Australia next year. I met some of Garth's buddies in the field called the "warlords." They were a group of miners who lived on the edge. They'd get up in the morning, smoke a little marijuana, mine a few hours, drink a lot of beer, mine some more, smoke some more, and eat once in a while. It made you wonder what kept them alive. One of them was a Vietnam vet who married an

Aborigine. After a fight one night, he got into his car and ran over her until she was dead and then buried her somewhere in the bush.

The Aussies were survivors and did everything by trial and error. If their car broke down, they, including the sheilas, would figure out how to fix the bloody thing and be on their way. They also built their own houses in the outback with whatever material was available—tin, logs, rocks, and so on. For water, they used tanks that filled with rainwater by gutters from the roof or were delivered from the nearest town. Electricity was supplied by generators. And cooking was done by with propane stoves.

One day, I road my motorcycle to Hebel, Queensland, about a hundred kilometers north of Lightning Ridge to return some parts I'd borrowed a month earlier. While I was there, I put a yabby (crawdad) trap in the river and then went to the pub for a beer. Well, after quite a few beers and good conversation with the locals, I got on that bike and went back to retrieve my trap but fell off and fractured my ankle and bruised a couple of ribs—all for only one yabby. Well, that was life in the outback.

Most Aborigines in town were easy to get along with. But the younger generation were educated agitators from the big cities and were stirring up the older groups by demanding land rights and percentages of the mining claims. I was afraid that, within ten years, there would be a revolution in Australia, and blood would flow. The situation here was very similar to the American Indians, whose land we took away from them. The Australians should have settled this dispute a long time ago, but we always think problems will eventually work themselves out. Only by then, it's too late. The Aborigines were given welfare and were allowed to own houses and automobiles without putting up any cash, which made them very lazy because they had no incentive to work.

The town got busy in March and September; people were either returning from summer coastal areas or selling their opals before the holidays. Mates wouldn't sell opals to mates because it created an uneasy feeling between each person, like maybe they didn't get a good deal.

Buying opal in the rough was the cheapest option, but you didn't know if there was any color. For a higher price, you could buy opal that had been rubbed (ground), so you see color but didn't know how much. But usually it all balanced out. If the rough contained a lot of crystal, you could make doublets or triplets by gluing the crystal with epoxy to a piece of black potch that brought out the color. These were valued less than solids, so remember, buyer beware.

I'd been cutting opals for a couple of months now, and in the afternoon when I went for a swim in the Olympic-sized pool the town had, I'd close my eyes and see an array of colors very few people had ever experienced. I individually bagged and weighed all three hundred opals, and Jim put a price on each one—some as much as A $300. Then we went into town and met Terry Lau from Hong Kong, who paid Jim his price less 20 percent. I figured I'd take the opals back to the United States and see what they'd be worth. Who knew?

I took Gus and Michele and Jim and his wife, Mim, to dinner at the LRBC and thanked them for giving me an opal experience. The next day, I bought a bus/train ticket for seventy-five dollars to Blacktown near the Richmond Royal Australian Air Force Base outside of Sydney. The night before I left, Gus, Michele, and I cooked some steaks on the barbie in his backyard with scotch and wine and a white tablecloth; it was the best night since I'd been here.

The next day, I secured the caravan at the Lightning Ridge Park and then hugged everyone and said goodbye. I took a bus to Dubbo, where I caught a train to Blacktown that took six hours, winding through the Blue Mountains. The train was clean, quiet, and roomy, with very friendly passengers, all wanting to know about America. I had a nice dinner with wine and then sat back and gazed at all those opals I'd cut. I couldn't believe it.

I arrived in Blacktown at seven o'clock that evening and then took a city train for a dollar to Windsor and then walked across the street to the Railway Saloon. No rooms were available, but after a couple of beers, Betty the bartender found me a room at Tropicana Motel near the Richmond RAAF for forty-eight dollars, including breakfast.

A flight was leaving Richmond in a few days, so I took the city train to Sydney and checked out the opal stores. The prices were five times those in Lightning Ridge. I took a ferry across Sydney Harbor and visited the Taronga Zoo and saw the largest gorilla family in captivity. When I got back to Windsor Train Station, I called the Tropicana, and the driver picked me up. On the way back to the motel, we stopped off for some fish and chips. These Aussies were great people.

I arrived at Richmond the next morning, and while I was going through customs, the officers found I had overstayed my visa by a month and stamped my passport for no further travel to Australia unless I wrote a letter to the consulate and explained the reason. I departed Richmond on a C-141 at ten o'clock in the morning and arrived at eight o'clock the night before in Pago Pago, American Samoa because of the dateline. After an hour of unloading cargo and refueling, we arrived at Hickam six hours later—at three o'clock the same morning we'd left Australia.

It was April, and the weather in Reno was still cold. So, I spent a week in Hawaii playing tennis, swimming, and working on my tan. One day, I went to the IRS to file for an extension on my taxes but found out you didn't have to sign the form anymore. I could have sent the extension from anywhere outside the country.

Because of Typhoon ISA off Japan, few flights were coming in. So, I caught a C-5 to McChord AFB, Tacoma, Washington, but was diverted to Elmendorf AFB, Anchorage, Alaska. It was eighty-two degrees when I left Hawaii and twenty-eight degrees when we arrived at Elmendorf; there I was in my shorts with a dark tan. The C-5 broke down, and I had to spend two days in nothing but a warmup suit. But I made the best of it, telling everyone at the O club about my trip to Australia.

They finally fixed the plane, and after a stop at McChord, I finally arrived at Travis and picked up my car at the long-term parking; after six months, it started right up.

On the way to Reno, I stopped off at Mi-Bo Jewelers in Rancho Cordova, and the jeweler said he would take all three hundred opals on consignment for two or three months. We agreed on a price, and I headed for Reno.

I relaxed during the summer, swimming and playing golf with a friend, Art Schmidt. We decided to play every course in Reno, Carson City, and Lake Tahoe, always looking for the best deals. One day, I met a gal at the Washoe Tennis Courts who'd just gotten a divorce and was living in an $800,000 house in Glenbrook at Lake Tahoe. We would drink and cook every night, and then I would chase her around that big house. But she would never let me get too close. One night, after a little too much to drink, I got frustrated and headed down the mountain in my Ranchero, missing a curve and hitting a guardrail. I wiped out the right side of my car, but after repairs and a complete paint job, the car looked as good as new. Women—fuck 'em!

Reno was a pleasant summer retreat, with temperatures rarely reaching a hundred degrees because it was at 4,500 feet. You could play golf or tennis; swim, fish, or sail; go hiking; or take a chance at losing your money at the casinos. The weather didn't warm up until June, but it stayed nice and clear into October. After that, though, watch out. An early storm could sneak in and catch you off guard. That was exactly what happened on October 21, 1997, so I packed my bags and got out of town.

I stopped at Mi-Bo's Jewelers in Rancho Cordova to check on my opals and sold fifty stones for $1,500 cash. Then I headed to Travis AFB near Fairfield, but there were very few flights, and the passenger terminal was full of people. So, I bought a ticket on American Trans Air from SFO to Honolulu via Maui for $187.

After leaving my car at the base and taking a shuttle to SFO, I departed that night on a Lockheed 1011. And after arriving in Honolulu, I rented a midsize car from Tradewinds for $550 a month and then drove around checking out the military billeting. I found a room at the Pearl Harbor Bachelor Officer Quarters for twenty dollars a night, had a swim, and then went to the Hickam O club for an all-you-could-eat seafood buffet for fifteen dollars. The next day, I went to DHTC and played tennis with all the snowbirds and then went to lunch at the Yum Yum Tree with Papa Joe Gladstone, an eighty-two-year-young tennis player from Winnipeg, Manitoba.

Eventually, I got down to Ala Moana Tennis Center to play with the locals and ran into Dr. Jerry Merkil and his wife, Sandy, from Reno. I showed him some opals, and he bought $1,200 worth. Maybe that trip to Australia was going to pay off after all.

I also played tennis at Kapiolani Park. Now, I'd made the rounds. You know the saying—absence makes the heart grow founder. Well, the players were always asking me where I'd been hanging out. One day, I was swimming some laps at the Hickam Pool, and there was a Chinese man about my age in the lane next to me. When we finished, we got to talking, and I found out he was President Jiang Zemin of China. You never knew who you were going to meet on these military bases.

I decided to check out the golf courses this trip, with the best ones located on military bases, where civilians guests were invited. The best kept secret was the Klipper Golf Course at the Marine Corps Base Hawaii (MCBH) at Kaneohe Bay on the east side of the island. It reminded me of Pebble Beach but for a tenth the cost. The BOQ there was quieter, cooler, and sat on top of a hill with a spectacular view of the ocean. So, I checked out of Pearl Harbor and got a room at MCBH, where the trade winds blew, and you didn't need an air conditioner.

The drive to Waikiki only took twenty-five minutes via the Pali Highway, which climbed to a thousand feet and crossed through the Koolau Mountains. It rained there 90 percent of the time, so I got a free car wash every day. I thought this island was small. But each time I came here, I learned of more places the tourists never heard about because they were always with a tour group.

The prices of condominiums are around $120,000. That was about $60,000 below what they had been a few years ago because the Japanese overbuilt in the 1980s and were having trouble unloading their properties. There were also plenty of job opportunities (tourism, hotel, restaurant, and such). Plus, young girls had come to the island and made good money in topless and bottomless bars. The governor was trying to clean things up, but the Japanese men would pay big bucks to be with an American blond. And Americans would do the same to be with an Asian girl. So it was a case of supply and demand.

The Hawaiian language, which consists of fourteen letters of our alphabet, had been forgotten for a hundred years and was being taught again in the public schools. Some words had dual meanings. *Aloha* means "hello" and "goodbye." And *mahalo* means "thank you" and "you're welcome."

CHAPTER 12

BACK TO AUSTRALIA

I'd had enough tennis. So, I caught a flight from Hickam AFB to Richmond RAAF via Christ Church, New Zealand, on a C-5 and then a train to Sydney. The weather was in the seventies and a little humid, and the city was under construction, getting ready for the 2000 Summer Olympics.

I found an ATM machine that automatically converted your money into Australian dollars, with the rate at A$1.50 to US$1 and dropping due to the sluggish economy in Asia. I took the train to Kings Cross and found a room for A$35. After a couple of days of relaxation, I bought a ticket on the CountryLink train to Dubbo and then a bus to Lightning Ridge, where I was met by my mates Gus and Michele. We had a feed (dinner) and got drunk. then I spent the night in my caravan that had been moved from the park to Gus's backyard.

The next day, I helped Gus change a tire on his drill rig and then moved it to another drill site; nothing had changed. Gus and I towed my caravan down to the pistol club, where I had electricity, a toilet, and a shower at the bore baths a quarter mile away—all for a dollar a day. I hauled water for drinking and cooking but only used about twenty liters a week. The best part of it all was that I was completely alone with just the emus, parrots, and kangaroos. But don't let those cute kangaroos fool you. They had been known to grab a cow with their small front paws and rip open its stomach with the large claws on their hind legs.

I saw Michael Smith, and he wanted me to work for him cutting opals because he had more work than he could handle. The atmosphere in Lightning Ridge had become a little sullen this year, with the price of opals dropping with the Asian market. A lot of miners who were just getting by last year had left town, and the rest were holding onto their opals until the prices changed, hopefully for the better.

Because of El Niño, the weather in some parts of Australia had become very hot and dry, especially in the southern portions. Sheep and cattle were dying, rivers and lakes were drying up, and families were leaving their ranches. But Australians are a hearty breed, and when the rains returned, the people would rebound. At Lightning Ridge, though, it was just the opposite.

One night, five inches of rain came down, and when I woke up the next morning, my caravan was surrounded by a lake. So, I opened a bottle of scotch and watched the Hopman Cup tennis tournament on television all day. I eventually dug a trench to drain some of the water. And after a few days, when the ground started drying up, I built a levee around my caravan, plus a graveled driveway so I could get in and out.

People in Australia maintain their friendship longer than they do in the United States. When an old miner died the other day, 750 people came to his funeral.

There were some insects that drove you crazy, like the flies. If you didn't wear a broad-brimmed hat, they'd fly in your eyes, in your ears, and up your nose. And the ants would bite or eat anything that stood still. There was a funnel spider that, if threatened, would jump and attack and had enough venom to kill a human. Then there was the fierce snake that was so aggressive it would chase you if aggravated it and had enough venom to kill twenty humans. The Aussies say, if you're camping, you should spread ashes from your fire around the campsite; snakes can't crawl over the ashes because they lose traction. Also you could put milk in an old soup can with the lid pushed inside; the snake would get its head caught, and you wouldn't get bit trying to kill it.

One day, I met Stuart, an opal miner, at the LRBC. He used to crew on the Sydney to Hobart Yacht Races and said he could get me on a boat returning from Hobart as a crew member.

It was the Christmas holidays again, and Gus, Michele, and I were going to dinner parties every day. But on Christmas night, after having a little too much to drink, I was riding my motorcycle back to my caravan when I was attacked by a dingo dog and flipped the bike. When I came to, the bike, the dog, and I were all tangled up together, and when I lifted the bike up, that dog took off running. If it wasn't for my helmet, it could have been more serious than it was, though I broke my collar bone, tore some cartilage in my right knee, burned my right ankle on the exhaust pipe, bruised some ribs, and scraped off a lot of skin. I managed to get the bike started and rode to my caravan, where I spent the night.

The next morning, I rode the bike three miles back to town to the hospital to have my shoulder and ribs wrapped and the wounds dressed. I tell you, if you didn't take care of yourself, you could die in the outback and nobody would know where you were. Because the doctor in Lightning Ridge was on vacation at the Gold Coast, Gus and I went to a hospital in Walgett, about an hour's drive away.

I met Sinead, a pretty radiologist from Ireland, who took pictures of my chest and shoulder and said she visits Lightning Ridge once a week, and we might get together. The doctor said the shoulder would heal, but I had to have my arm bandaged to my chest to reduce movement.

Gus and Michele told me to get rid of that bike and buy a car. So, we found a Holden, like a Chevrolet, for four hundred dollars. It was an automatic, so I could at least drive with my left hand. But because the steering wheel was on the right, my depth perception was off, and I kept hitting trees around my caravan with the left fender.

Now I was the target at the bowling club for razzing and jokes because of the bike accident and my bad driving in that Holden. But hell, I was just a goddamn one-armed yank. I was also hearing stories of miners who'd had worse accidents than me and were lucky to be alive to talk about them.

I found a therapist in Walgett who had been stretching my shoulder regardless of how much it hurt because, if it wasn't stretched now, it would restrict movement for the rest of my life.

It had been three weeks since the accident. And since I was in no shape to mine, cut opals, or sail, I decided to travel around the country while my body healed itself. I left Lightning Ridge for Dubbo and then took a train south to Melbourne in Victoria, arriving on January 19, 1998, for the first day of the Australian Open. The city reminded me of San Francisco, cold and windy because of the Bass Strait, which brought in the cold winds. The tournament, located in Melbourne Park, was very well organized, and for only A$15, you could walk around all day watching any matches except the stadium court. After two weeks, John Korda from the Czech Republic and Martina Hingis from Switzerland took home the titles.

I took a twelve-hour train ride to Adelaide in South Australia for A$45. Adelaide was like San Diego, warm and friendly. I checked into the Motel Adjacent Casino downtown for A$39 a night and met the owners, David and Diana, who also treated me like family. I walked down to Rundle Street and discovered three blocks of restaurants with food from all over the world. So, I sampled a different place every night.

Also within walking distance was the Adelaide Cricket Club, which had one of the most picturesque cricket ovals in Australia. The games started at nine o'clock in the morning and usually lasted until sundown, with teams playing up to three hours without a break.

David, Diana, and I went to the Strathmore Restaurant one night, and I had "Meat on a Hot Rock." The dish consisted of kangaroo, a lean, dry meat; emu, a red, rich, moist meat; and crocodile, which had a very bland chicken-like taste.

It was January 26, Australia Day, when Australia became a nation in 1850. The day is celebrated like the Fourth of July in the United States. David and his staff had a barbie on the roof of his eight-story motel, where we drank, ate, and watched a fireworks show.

The dead skin on my burned ankle was still not healing, so I went to a plastic surgeon, who grafted skin from my thigh. That laid me up in St Andrews Hospital for a couple of days. The best part about the hospital stay was that, every morning, two pretty nurses would come into my room and give me a bed bath.

When I left the hospital, David had a room at his motel ready for me with beer in the icebox—what great people here. I took a tour around Adelaide Hills, similar to Napa County, and tasted some of the best wines in Australia. Next, I visited the quaint little town of Victor Harbor, which had the only horse-drawn rail trolley in the world. The trolley took you to Granite Island, where small penguins lived.

The next day I went to Kangaroo Island on a high-speed catamaran to observe a variety of wildlife and visited a sheep ranch, where I learned the art of shearing, which requires a lot of backbreaking work. Professionals could shear up to a hundred sheep a day, making about A$1.50 per sheep. But many didn't last more than a year or so.

The next day, while hiking on a sea lion beach, my knee started giving out. When I returned to Adelaide, an orthopedic surgeon said I had torn cartilage from that motorcycle accident and needed surgery. The operation only took an hour, and I was out of the Adelaide Day Surgery that afternoon but had to use crutches for about a week.

One day, I bought five kilos of blue swim crabs, French bread, and wine. Then I took David and Diana for a picnic that evening along the Torrens River. The next weekend, David invited me up to his cabin retreat on the Murray River with his family and friends for water skiing, cricket, a barbie, and a lot of beer. I finally went for my first swim since the accident. That therapist in Walgett had been right about stretching—what a great feeling.

It was time to move on. So, I bought ten thousand kilometers on the Greyhound Pioneer Australia for A$600 and decided to tour the country. The buses had toilets, air-conditioning, videos, and reclining seats, much like the airlines. You could get off and on the bus anytime. So, my first stop was Port Augusta, north of Adelaide, where I rented a car for a day and drove to Flinders Ranges. I found Aboriginal caves at Yourambulla with three thousand-year-old hieroglyphic paintings that showed how the Aborigines had lived, what they'd eaten, and where they'd migrated.

I spent the night at the Prairie Hotel in Parachilna and met some true outback Aussies in the bar, where we drank beer, ate camel and goat meat, and told jokes all night. Not a bad place to live, no worries.

The next day, I drove through Brachina Gorge and Wilpena Pound and discovered 800 million year old rock formations. Then I drove back to Augusta and spent the night at the Flinders Hotel for a nice dinner. The next morning, I boarded the Greyhound to Coober Pedy and checked into Radeka's Motel for A $50 and stayed in a room that was built underground because the temperature during the day reached 50 degrees Celsius (130 degrees Fahrenheit) but with a comfortable 72 degrees Fahrenheit in my room.

Coober Pedy, north of Port Augusta, was also an opal mining town like Lightning Ridge but produced white opals, more commonly seen in the United States. The town used to haul water to town by trucks, which made a quart bottle cost four dollars, but they'd since found an aquifer under the town and pumped water through a desalination plant that removed the salt by electrolysis but left just enough chlorine.

I left Coober Pedy on the Greyhound for the Northern Territory to Ayres Rock, (Uluru). the most visited site in Australia, it received a thousand people a day. The rock is the largest monolith in the world, extending a thousand feet high and a mile long. Uplifted and tilted, it then eroded and looked like a loaf of bread that turned red during the sunset due to the iron content. A resort near the rock offered lodging ranging from campsites to a five-star hotel, with restaurants where you could have anything from a hamburger to fresh lobster flown in by commercial airlines.

I left Ayers Rock the next day for Alice Springs, a tourist oasis in the center of Australia, where I swam, played tennis, and ate at some great restaurants. The Greyhound picked me up, and I headed north toward Darwin on a ten-hour trip that took me from a hot, dry desert climate to a wet, humid tropical zone. One of our many stops en route was Wycliffe Wells, a roadside café, bar, and gas station that claimed to have been visited by UFOs in 1965 and had replicated flying saucers and little green men to try and prove the point.

I arrived in Darwin and checked into the Poinciana Hotel for A$52, half the regular rate due to the wet season, which extended from November through April. Darwin, which had a population of fifteen thousand, was a very modern fishing and tourism town, rebuilt due to the destruction it received from the Japanese during World War II and Cyclone Tracy in 1974. Most of the tourists I met were staying at backpacking lodges, cooking their own meals to save money for the local tours. But Greyhound offered me the same tours for a tenth the price. So, I spent the money I saved on nice hotels and fine restaurants.

I went on a $400 two-day trip to Kakadu National Park for $40 and had to get around by boat or plane because of the wet season. But the waterfalls were magnificent. I observed a saltwater crocodile that was able to leap its full five-meter (fifteen-foot) length out of the water to catch meat held above it by local Australians. The park also abounded with Aboriginal art and teemed with wildlife. There were sea eagles, silver-crested cockatoos, and long-neck turtles and, of course, a lot of crocs. The difference between freshwater and saltwater crocs is the freshwater croc has a long, thin snout with a bump on the end and is very timid toward humans, but the "salty," that lives in both fresh water and salt water is bigger and darker, with a wider mouth, and aggressive enough to approach humans near riverbanks and drag them under.

After a few days, I took the Greyhound west to the town of Kununurra in Western Australia, where the terrain was getting more rugged and the climate less tropic. Kununurra had about seven thousand people and was built in 1964 because of the Ord River. Fed by Lake Argyle, the river produced great soil and irrigation for crops ranging from pineapples to cotton. And the place was free of insects because the bugs hadn't discovered the area yet. South of the lake was the Argyle Diamond Mine, which opened in 1985 and produced rare pink diamonds worth ten to fifty times that of white diamonds.

Argyle mined 35 million carats per year and employed seven hundred personnel who worked twelve-hour shifts for two weeks and then were flown to Perth, where they lived, for a week off. The workers make an average of A$70,000 a year and were strictly watched by the mine, with very thorough random searches for diamond theft. The diamonds were flown to the main headquarters in Perth, sorted, and priced and then sent to Bombay, India, and Brussels, Belgium, for cutting.

The life of the mine was expected to end in 2004, making pink diamonds a good investment. So, I brought two twenty-six-point pink champagne brilliant cut diamonds back with me, worth about $5,000 each.

Since I'd been to Perth, I decided this was the farthest west I was going. So, I took the Greyhound back to Alice Springs via Katherine, a town at the mouth of a beautiful gorge that floods the town every forty years. In fact, Katherine was recovering from a flood that had hit a couple of months ago, leaving the town under seven feet of water.

After leaving Alice Springs at night, we hit and killed four kangaroos on the way to Adelaide because, when they saw headlights, the kangaroos would just stop and stare. Most cars were equipped with roo bars, so collisions with the animals didn't damage the front end of their vehicles.

I checked back into the Adjacent Casino motel and got pissed (drunk) with David and Diana that night and barely got up in time to catch the Greyhound out of town to Dubbo. After spending the night, I took the CountryLink to Lightning Ridge and met Gus at the LRBC for a schooner of cold beer and told him about my trip. I used up just about all of the ten thousand kilometers I'd bought in Adelaide two months ago, costing me six cents per kilometer to travel around Australia.

While I was gone, Michele had blown the engine on my Holden, driving four hundred kilometers a day making money shuttling old people around the state. She'd had an old engine put in, but the car ran like shit. So, I replaced the fuel pump, carburetor, and a transmission seal. Michele was upset with me because I was spending money on the Holden. Apparently, Aussies wouldn't pay to have things fixed unless they actually broke, whereas I believed in preventive maintenance.

I went to a barbie at Sandy's folks. I'd met Sandy last year but now found out that she'd turned lesbian and her brother had contracted the AIDS virus; and I thought my life was screwed up.

I joined the pistol club and started competing, shooting a Ruger .22. But since Australia has very strict gun laws, including requiring permits for BB guns, I had trouble getting a license.

It was Easter weekend, and the town had its twenty-second annual goat race. People brought wild goats to town and hitched them to two-wheeled carts driven by young lads. Each goat was paraded in front of the crowd for a bidding auction to see who got to bet on the goat. Then four groups at a time raced until there is one winner left. Most of the goats were uncontrollable and either wound up in the crowd or hit a tree or car going at full speed; miraculously nobody and no goat were seriously hurt.

After laughing at those goats, we finally adjourned to the bowling club for a big raffle and a lot of cold beer. And would you believe I won three packages of meat, enough to feed Gus and Michele for a month?

It was April, and the nights are becoming cooler. So maybe I'd head back to Hawaii. The only problem was Gus and Michele sensed I was getting restless and were trying to keep me from leaving. Aussies become very emotionally attached, and it was difficult to say goodbye.

I left Lightning Ridge on April 21 for Richmond RAAF via Dubbo, Parramatta City, where the convicts first arrived from England and Windsor—only to arrive and find out that the C-141 going to Hickam, Hawaii, had broken down. I obtained a military discount ticket on Air New Zealand for A$540 to Honolulu via Auckland and Fiji. The trains to Sydney stopped running at midnight, so I arrived that night for my flight that left at seven o'clock the next morning. Unfortunately, the airport closed from midnight to four o'clock. So, I slept outside the terminal on a bench with other travelers, no worries.

I left Sydney in a B-767 to Auckland and then took a B-747 to Honolulu via a quick stop in Nadi, Fiji, arriving at four o'clock in the morning twelve hours later that same day. I rented a car and then saw the tennis gang at Ala Moana, who were envious of my lifestyle. Either they were married, or they couldn't afford to travel. I hit balls for the first time since I'd dislocated my shoulder and started swimming in the ocean, which seems to heel me up faster—must be the salt water.

Had a free mai tai that night at the Royal Hawaiian from my bartender friend Sam Uta, who couldn't believe what I'd been through since I'd last seen him. I stayed in Hawaii for a month playing tennis and golf and swimming all for about thirty dollars a day—what a life.

I caught a C-5 back to Travis and then drove to Reno, encountering snow at six thousand feet over Donner Summit; and it was already the end of May. Nothing had changed in Reno. Everybody had cabin fever from the past winter and couldn't stand it when I showed up with a tan.

My brother had passed away last March with cancer in the liver and yellow jaundice due to bad eating habits and a lack of exercise. He was only fifty-eight years old and was a workaholic so he could buy all his toys but never enjoyed them.

I played golf and tennis and swam in Reno for a couple of months. Then I went to Travis and caught a C-141 to McChord AFB, Tacoma, Washington. I rented a car and drove up to Abbotsford, British Columbia, to spend a week with a tennis friend of mine who I'd met in Hawaii.

Abbotsford was in a lush green valley, where farmers grew a lot of raspberries, which I couldn't get enough of. We played tennis every day and drank and chased girls every night, with everyone envious of me because I got CAN$1.50 for US$1. The people weren't rude, but they didn't care much for Americans because they thought we flaunted our prosperity.

After a week, I drove down to Whidbey Island Naval Air Station via Interstate 5 and the Mukilteo Ferry through Puget Sound. I spent the night at the BOQ for nine dollars and had a great prime rib dinner for nine dollars and then drove back to McChord the next day. I caught a C-9 medivac flight to Travis and then drove up the hill, arriving in Reno at six o'clock that evening, just in time for a cocktail.

CHAPTER 13

NEW ZEALAND

I had a $10,000 surgery done on my nasal passage in December 1998 at Stanford Medical Center in Palo Alto through the Veterans Administration. It cost me absolutely nothing; being a military veteran sure paid off. I drove down to Tucson, Arizona, for the holidays and stayed at Nellis AFB, Las Vegas; Edwards AFB, California; Luke AFB, Phoenix; Davis Monthan AFB, Tucson; and Marine Corps Air Station, Yuma—all for twelve dollars a night plus cheap golf.

I met a lovely girl named Chi on the tennis courts at Ft. Lowell Park in Tucson, and she invited me to her country club at Westward Look for a week, where I swam, sunned, and played tennis with her friends. The city was very clean, with friendly people and great winter weather and a low cost of living with few Mexicans because they all migrated to Phoenix; maybe it was time to move out of Reno.

I visited the Biosphere 2 forty miles south of Tucson. A simulated enclosed environment built for life on another planet and with four seasons, Biosphere 2 costing an oil tycoon $300 million to build and $8 million a year to operate.

After Christmas I drove to Palm Springs and called Max Baker. A tennis friend of mine from Reno, Max was staying at a condo at the Desert Princess Resort, where I stayed playing tennis and golf until the first of the year. I drove back to Reno for a month and then flew back and forth to Hawaii three times from February through April, spending nearly two months on the beaches and tennis courts in Waikiki.

The rest of the summer was spent in Reno, until November 1999, when the weather started getting cold. I called the Reno Air National Guard and found out they had a flight leaving for Hickam November 17. On a cold, thirty-six degree, overcast morning, I left my car covered at home, took a taxi to the Reno International Airport, and caught a C-130 to Travis for refueling. Then I was on to Hawaii, arriving nine hours later because of headwinds and those slow turboprop engines.

All the billeting was full, so I rented a car from VIP for $500 a month, drove over the Pali Highway to the MCBH in Kaneohe, and checked into the BOQ for $25 a day. Art, a seventy-five-year-old friend of mine from Reno wanted to come to Hawaii next month and share a condo. So, the next day, I checked the classified ads but couldn't find anything for less than a six-month lease. I drove to DHTC and saw Papa Joe and the gang at the tennis courts, and someone said to check with Beachcomber Realty located in the Landmark Building on Kalakaua and Ala Wai. Alice, the broker, had a one-bedroom, one-bath, full kitchen, washer/dryer, and lanai at the Pavilion across the street for $900 a month, which was $500 less than the average price in Waikiki.

After spending the rest of the month playing tennis at Ala Moana, swimming at the beach, and working out at Semper Fitness Center at MCBH, I moved into the Pavilion on December 2. I picked up Art at the airport and then we went to the Pearl Harbor Commissary and bought two weeks' worth of food, saving up to 50 percent of Hawaii prices.

Art hadn't been here since 1945 and only remembered the Royal Hawaiian and Moana Loa Hotels in Waikiki, which you couldn't even see now because of all the high-rises built since the late 1960s. I introduced Art to Diamond Head, Ala Moana, and Kapiolani courts. He preferred DHTC because of the European and Canadian tourists, including Papa Joe, who was eighty-three years old but didn't look a day over seventy.

One night, I took Art to the Hickam Officers' Club for the best king crab he had ever tasted. The next morning, we saw four thousand Harleys from our lanai going to Waikiki for a "toys for tots" parade. Later that day, we drove to the West Locks near Pearl Harbor, where Art had been on a ship fifty-five years ago. Then we went up the west coast to check out the surfers at Makaha Beach. I introduced him to ahi (tuna) and moonfish at Kincaid's in the Ward Shopping Center that night, and he was impressed; it was obvious he didn't eat enough fish.

One day, we went to Sunset Beach to watch Sunny Garcia, Andy Irons, and the boys surf fifteen-foot-plus waves at the Pipeline in the International Masters Surf Contest. The waves were so high jet skis would tow the surfers so they could pick up enough speed. It took a rare surfer to ride those waves.

One morning, 27,000 runners went by our lanai for the Annual Honolulu Marathon, the fourth largest in the world. The race 5:00 a.m., with the last runner finishing around sunset. I took Art to MCBH Klipper Golf Course, which had three holes along the ocean and was prettier than Pebble Beach for a tenth the price.

Well, Art's two weeks were up. So, I took him to the airport for his flight back to Reno. He said he'd never felt so healthy in his life—must be the salt air and the hula girls.

On New Year's Eve the wind died down, and the air got so smoky from the fireworks you had to stay inside. The police confiscated fifteen tons of fireworks and were now trying to figure out how to dispose of the cargo.

Because there were very few military airlift command MAC flights going south, I bought a discount ticket from SATO to New Zealand for $600 round trip. I cleaned the condo; left the keys with the manager; and called Alice, who said she would have a condo for me when I returned. Then I took the number 19 bus to the airport. Because of terrorist threats from Osama bin Laden, the security at Honolulu International was very tight and irritating. I wished I was flying on a MAC flight.

I left Hawaii at one o'clock in the morning on January 18, 2000, on an Air Pacific B-767-300ER, arriving nine hours later in Nadi, Fiji. I spent most of the flight in the cockpit with the Fijian crew, talking about our flying experiences. Fiji comprises about three hundred islands, growing mainly sugar cane. And the Fijians, like the Hawaiians, have their own language. I arrived in Auckland, New Zealand, about two and a half hours later at ten o'clock in the morning to overcast skies with light rain showers and temperatures in the seventies.

I used my ATM card at the airport and received $1.90 for my dollar and then took a shuttle to Grafton Hall, where I got a room with community baths and breakfast for NZ$32 (US$17) a day. I walked to the ASB Bank Tennis Center and just missed the Heineken Open two days ago, when Magnus Norman defeated Michael Chang in the finals. I met Sam Pehi, a Maori who invited me to his tennis club the next day for some doubles with his friends.

Grafton Hall mostly housed university students. And my nineteen-year-old next-door neighbor, Tracey Wilson, said she would show me around the town one day. Auckland is nicknamed "the City of Sails" because it has more sailboats per capita than anywhere else in the world. And the city was hosting the America's Cup this year. The semifinals had just finished. The United States had lost to Italy and was scheduled to sail against New Zealand next month. It seemed like I was just missing events by a few days.

The next day, Sam picked me up and we went to the Ngatara Tennis Club and played on artificial grass with sand, which made footing very slippery unless you had special soles on your shoes. Sam, who was sixty-eight years old, was very physically fit and looked younger because of his Polynesian descent. He owned a liquor store in the city and a club in Sydney, where he spent half his time. After tennis, I started to shake hands with everyone, but they pulled my face toward them, and we touched noses and foreheads together. That was the Maori way of saying you are a good friend; hell, I thought they were going to kiss me.

That night, Tracey and I had dinner. Then she drove me in her Morris Mini to Mount Eden, where we had a 360-degree view of Auckland. The next morning, I walked to Kiwi Experience and bought a NZ$675 ticket for a three-week tour of both the North and South Islands in a forty-passenger bus. You could get off and on anywhere you wanted and stay as long as you desired.

The next day I took a ferry to Waiheke Island and found Palm Beach, where people enjoyed the sun and surf in the nude. I met two girls on the beach, and it was very difficult to look them in the eye while we were talking, especially with New Zealand women being so full breasted. And of course they kept kidding me about my tan line, which they didn't have.

The Kiwi Bus picked me up the following morning outside my hotel, and when I got on, it was full of young backpacking college kids. I guess there was another bus company that had an older crowd—oh well. Hamish, the driver, was forty years old and somewhat knowledgeable about the country but acted younger because of the kids on board. Our first stop was Hot Water Beach, where you dug a hole in the sand and sat in it and enjoyed the therapeutic relief from the hot thermal water seeping up.

We spent the first night in Coromandel, where I had to share a room in a backpacking lodge with five kids without sheets, blankets, or towels because all the kids had their sleeping bags. The next day, we went south to Rotorua, where a high concentration of Maori lived. I finally found a motel away from those kids and then went to the Aquatic Park and swam a mile.

I met a geologist who said Rotorua was on a large thermal deposit that was so active houses would disappear on occasions from the ground giving way, and the steam was so hot the Maori would cook their food in the hot pools around town. That evening, we were invited to a Maori tribe that served us pork and fowl that had been cooked in hot rock pits covered with burlap. Then after the feast, they put on a demonstration of their native dances.

There was a volcanic crater lake nearby called Taupo that had some of the largest trout in the world, weighing up to forty pounds. Our next stop was Tongariro, where I went on a seven-hour hike from Mangatepopo to a crater 1,700 meters (5,300 feet) above sea level. On my way back down the mountain. after separating myself from the rest of the crowd. I stopped to reload my camera and a karearea falcon landed about five feet away and watched me. But as soon as I got the film in, he took off. I guess he wanted to be left alone, like I did. What a magnificent experience. All I could remember were the large pupils in his eyes as he was staring at me. I wonder what he was thinking.

I went out for a lasagna dinner that night with a bottle of wine. I brought all for about NZ$35. There is a plant in New Zealand called Maseuka that, when made into tea, heals anything from common colds to severe stomach cramps.

The next day, we stopped in Whakapapa and observed the Grand Chalet, a 125-room hotel built in 1923 that survived a massive volcanic eruption that destroyed an entire ski resort about fifty years ago. We spent the night in a ranch house on the Rangitikei River. The kids went rafting, and Hamish and I played a nine-hole golf course in a forest with a pitching wedge and a putter. Not only did you lose your balls but you also got lost just trying to find the next hole.

We finally arrived in Wellington, the capital of New Zealand located on the south end of the North Island, with a population of 250,000, the third largest following Auckland and Christchurch. The two islands were separated by Cook Strait, created by numerous faults, making the weather and surrounding landscape in Wellington similar to San Francisco. I found one of many fine restaurants in town and treated myself to blue point oysters, a rack of lamb, and a bottle of Rosemount Shiraz from Australia.

The next day, the bus spent three hours on a ferry in rough seas going across the strait. So, I took a twenty-five-minute flight in a 1959 Aero Commander that was held together with spit and glue.

The South Island was greener and had more mountains than the North Island, making it an outdoorsmen paradise. New Zealanders' intimate connection with the land and their pride in their unique identity was symbolized by an emerging national emblem, the fern. The national parks were very clean because of such signs as, "Whatever you bring into our forests, please take out," and, "Use your own firewood, not our trees."

I met the Kiwi Bus and then we headed for the town of Nelson as the weather started changing for the worst; in fact. it rained all over New Zealand, including snow on Mount Cook; and it was supposed to be summer.

There were many placer gold mining towns on the South Island because of the high mountain peaks that caused gold runoff, which could be panned out in the streams below. We arrived at Franz Josef Glacier, where I rented boots, crampons (cleats), and an ice pick and took an eight-hour hike up some very challenging crevasses. The three hundred-meter thick glacier is the world's steepest and fastest-flowing commercially guided glacier in the world and was formed from Mount Cook, the highest mountain in New Zealand at 3,754 meters (11,600 feet). The hike ended with a relaxing evening in town at a local pub for pizza, beer, and billiards, making Franz Josef Glacier the most memorable part of the trip.

I met Damien Rico from France, who spoke fairly good English, and Jodi Larson from British Columbia. Both were older and more mature than the rest of the college kids on the bus. Damien and I would share a room during our stops for the night, not only making it cheaper for me but also making it so Damien didn't have to bunk in a room with a bunch of kids. Damien was a thirty-five-year-old part-time actor in Arras, France who looked up to me as his mentor; in fact, he kept calling me Daddy.

After crossing a mountain range, we arrived in Makarora in a dry desert valley, where it was warm. And this time of year, the sun didn't set until ten o'clock at night. After spending the night in an A-frame at a campsite, we headed south, passing Wanaka Lake, the largest lake in New Zealand. Then we went to Kawarau Bridge, where people were lined up waiting to bungee jump 45 meters (145 feet) to the river below. I decided against it because a doctor I'd met a few days earlier said a great deal of stress and pressure was put on the heart and the eyes while hanging upside down. I guess that didn't frighten most of the tourists. In fact, a week later, super tennis star Steffi Graf, who was touring around with Andre Agassi, gave it a try.

We arrived that evening in Queensland the gateway to Fiordland National Park, an endless area of sounds that draw water from the Antarctic. I checked into a single room with two bunk beds at the Pinewood Inn for NZ$30, with shared bath, kitchen, and lounge.

Damien paid me NZ$15 a night to stay in one of the beds without the inn knowing; plus, he was a hell of a cook.

We packed a lunch one day, including wine, and went on a two and a half-hour hike to Ben Lomond, 1,748 meters above the town. We enjoyed a spectacular panoramic view of Queensland. Then we traversed the mountain range for five hours, circling the town. Damien was impressed with my conditioning and couldn't believe I was fifty-eight years old and finally quit calling me Daddy. We finished the day off with a bottle of scotch and a home-cooked pasta dinner that Damien made and then went into town and chased the girls. The next day, we rented a right-hand drive car for NZ$50 each and drove three hundred kilometers to Milford Sound, where we took a ferry through a magnificent fiord with waterfalls, sheer cliff formations, glaciers, and fur seals. On our drive back to Queensland, we picked up a Korean student hitchhiker who had been waiting for five hours in the cold, wet weather for a ride—what a patient man.

I left Queensland on the Kiwi Bus after three days with our driver Hamish, who'd also stayed behind, and our first stop was Lake Pukaki. The lake had an extraordinary aqua color from the glacier and limestone runoff from Mount Cook. The country along the east side of the Southern Alps was very arid, similar to Nevada and agriculture areas like the San Joaquin Valley in California.

We arrived in Christchurch, a laid-back town that reminded me of Adelaide, where everything was within walking distance and the transportation was either by bus or trolley, unlike Auckland. Auckland was similar to Sydney, which was spread out, and everyone owned an automobile just to get around. The weather in Christchurch was very mild, and the people were friendly and helpful. So, Damien and I toured the museums and botanical garden with a couple of girls from Sweden who were on our bus and then had a pasta dinner with them at our hotel.

Christchurch had a military airfield where MAC flights came in from Hickam en route to Australia. The next day, I took a city bus to Brieton Beach for a little sun and surf and then met Damien at the Le

Bob Bolli Restaurant for a French dinner that Damien said wasn't as good as eating in his home country.

Well, Damien and I had had it with those kids on the bus. So, he bought an airline ticket to Sydney, and I bought an airline ticket to Auckland, where I arrived an hour later and then took a shuttle back to Grafton Hall, checking into the same room next to Tracey, who was glad to see me. We went out for dinner to Some Place Else, a great pub located in the Sheraton Auckland Hotel, where I had a glass of Famous Grouse scotch that was very smooth and tasty. The next day, I took the ferry back to Palm Beach on Waiheke Island for some more total tanning. Most New Zealanders stayed out of the sun because of a large hole in the ozone layer that had been growing for the past twenty years and let in a lot of ultraviolet rays.

I still had the rest of the island north of Auckland left on my Kiwi Bus ticket, so I got back on the bus. But this time, both the driver and passengers were more mature, making the trip much more enjoyable. We arrived in Pahia, a small, quiet beach town near the Bay of Islands on the north end of the North Island. I checked into the Mouse Trap Backpackers, a converted house with two kitchens and two lounges and a single room for myself for NZ$40 a night and met Monique, a gracious host, who made me feel at home with her French hospitality and sexy accent.

The next day, I took a ferry to Russell Peninsula and then hiked down to Long Beach, where I found a secluded beach to work on my total tan. Living expenses here were cheaper than anywhere in New Zealand, and the people were friendlier and very inquisitive about the United States. The weather year-round was warmer because it was only thirty degrees south of the equator. And if I ever decided to move to New Zealand, this would be the place.

The next day, I hitched a ride out of town to the Waitangi Golf Course and played eighteen holes with an engineer from Taiwan, who had rented a motor coach for twenty-five dollars a day and was traveling the islands on his own. Later that day, I toured a Maori settlement, where I saw the famous Ngatokimatawhaorua eighty-man warrior canoe. The canoe was hand-carved from the kauri tree. Four hundred years ago, the Maori warriors would row out into the Bay of Islands to protect the island from the attacking Spaniards. In fact, once a year, they still went out for a day and celebrated the event, occasionally overturning the canoe.

I hated to leave, but I had a flight booked to Hawaii in a few days. So, I took the Kiwi Bus back to Auckland and then a three-hour ferry ride to Great Barrier Island. The water en route was so rough passengers were tossed about the cabin, to the point that one woman almost dropped her child. We moored at Tryphena Harbor, where I met a bus that took me for a wild ride to Pohutukawa Lodge, located in a dense rain forest. I checked into a bungalow that was so hidden you couldn't see it until you were fifty feet away. The island was a getaway for the city folk who wanted to fish, hike, or just hide out from the crowd.

After a fresh snapper dinner and some Irish stout that night, I took a forty-minute flight to Auckland the next morning on a twin-engine Islander. I checked into the Grand Chancellor Hotel and relaxed by the pool for the day and then went to the bar for a scotch that included free hors d'oeuvres and great conversation with the ladies. After some raw oysters, a rack of lamb, and a bottle of Hardy's Shiraz, I slept like a rock. The room included free breakfast and a free shuttle to the airport the next morning, and after a NZ$20 departure fee, I boarded an Air Pacific B-767 to Nadi for a short layover. Then I was on to Honolulu through a storm that extended up to fifty thousand feet, making it impossible to avoid. I landed at Honolulu International at two o'clock in the morning. I took a taxi to Pearl Harbor and checked into the BOQ for twenty-five dollars and got a good rest.

Later that day, I called Alice at Beachcomber Realty, and she had a studio for me at the Hawaiian Monarch for $700 a month—what a gal. The room was on the thirty-fifth floor with a great view but was a little small and compacted with no lanai. I guess the Japanese tourists were used to that kind of cramped living.

I walked to DHTC for some tennis but was a little rusty. Then I saw Papa Joe, who gave me his senior bus pass that he didn't use. The only problem was his birth date said 1907; I hoped I wouldn't get caught. I went to Ala Moana and decided that swimming at the beach there was because the waves were separated by a reef, and there were markers every five hundred meters and no sharks. I bought a Wilson Hyper Carbon 4.3 tennis racquet from McCully Bike for $200; it seemed lighter and more powerful than my old Hammer.

After a month in that shoebox at the Hawaiian Monarch, Alice found me a bigger studio with a small kitchen and a large lanai at the Island Colony for the same price. I was on the twenty-second floor with a view of Diamond Head, the International Market Place, the Royal Hawaiian Hotel, Waikiki Beach, and the Ala Wai Golf Course.

I met Sushi, my next door neighbor, an insurance salesman in Japan studying English in Hawaii for six months. He was also a tennis player, so I invited him to Ala Moana. When he showed up, he had a pretty Japanese girl, Kaori, with him. She was in his English class and also played tennis. I took her and her girlfriend out to dinner one night, and they spoke just enough English that we got along great. Plus they felt safe with me, hanging onto my arms as we walked through Waikiki. The Japanese women were a little naive, showing off their newly learned English and were easily duped by American men.

One night, a couple of men followed a Japanese girl they met to her hotel room and then raped and robbed her. In fact, someone knocked on my door one night, and thinking it was Sushi, I opened the door. Two men were staring at me. When I asked them what they wanted, one of them said, "You know what we want," and proceeded to force their way into my room. Well, I shoved on that door as hard as I could, barely getting it closed, and immediately called security. But by the time security arrived, the men were gone. One guard took off down the stairs. The other one went up the stairs. And I went down to the lobby in the elevator. But they got away; next time, I'd know better.

It was getting toward the end of April, and the weather in Reno was warming up. So, I told the crowd at Ala Moana I was leaving. And would you believe it? They threw a going-away barbecue for me in the park near the tennis courts. That night, a couple of the tennis players took me to some local karaoke bars, where I had to mind my manners. I was the only haole there, and those Hawaiians were too big for me.

The next morning, Tommy Okino, Minako, and Johanna took me to lunch. I had my first Portuguese soup, which the place only made once a month. I checked out of the Island Colony; took a ten-dollar shuttle to Hickam; and caught a C-5 to Travis, even though my car was in Reno. I met a retired navy chief, along with his wife and daughter, on the flight. They lived in Carson City and offered me a ride. I filled his gas tank, and when we got to Reno, I was dropped off right in front of my door. This opportunity would never have happened outside the military.

CHAPTER 14

HAWAII

The summer of 2000 in Reno was uneventful. I spent it playing tennis, golf, swimming and riding my bike, just trying to keep healthy. I accumulated seven loans through Tilly and could now live off the interest without working; I wished I'd done this twenty years ago. It was October. So, I called the Reno Air National Guard. And would you believe it? There was a flight leaving for Hickam, Hawaii, in a couple of weeks.

I winterized my trailer, covered my car, and then caught a C-130 Hercules at 0730 to Travis AFB for fuel and then an eight-hour flight to Hawaii, arriving at 1430 Hawaiian time. I rented a car from Enterprise for $150 a week and then checked into the Pearl Harbor BOQ and took a swim and got some sun at Scott Pool. The next day, I called around for a condo in the $500 to $700 a month range. But each time I thought I found something, either the condo or the location was not very nice.

I went to Ala Moana for tennis and met Loren, a Korean schoolteacher looking for a husband; I wasn't sure how long this relationship was going to last. The next day, she invited me for tennis at Pearl Harbor and then to an admiral's beach cottage at Barbers Point Naval Air Station, where I met the admiral's sister, her daughter, another schoolteacher, and three other women. Well, needless to say, being the only man there, we had a great time swimming in the ocean, playing on the secluded beach, and then finishing the day with a barbecue—all for free.

I moved to the MCBH BOQ in Kaneohe Bay, where it was cooler and quieter, and the trade winds always blew. After a couple of days, I called Alice. She found me a one-bedroom condo at the Waikiki Park Heights located on Kuhio Avenue, just two blocks from the beach with a view of the sunset for $800 a month. Since, I'd given the rental car back. I rented out my parking space at the condo for $60 a month. I met my next-door neighbors on the lanai and found out they were from Kansas and paying $1,600 a month for the same condo through a travel agency. Again, it's who you know.

There was a kid down the street renting surfboards for $75 a week, compared to $10 an hour for rentals at Waikiki Beach. So, I thought, *What the hell? It's time I learn how to ride a wave.* The next morning, I took a ten-foot board to Waikiki and plunged into the water, only to discover I couldn't balance myself on that board. Every time I tried to catch a wave, I couldn't build up enough speed. After about three hours, a Hawaiian paddled over and said he'd been watching me for some time and that I looked perplexed. His name was Big Todd, and he was a surfing instructor on the beach. Big Todd told me I could spend all day out here and never catch a wave because the board was too short and too thin. So, I told him I would be back the next morning for a lesson.

When I woke up, I could barely get out of bed. Apparently, I'd bruised my ribs from paddling incorrectly on a board that was too short for me. I'd thought I was saving some money, but it cost me three weeks of healing time before I could get back to see Big Todd.

He started me on the sand on a twelve-foot, thick "longboard," showing me how to paddle and stand when I finally got a wave. Well, that board was like a Cadillac in the water—very stable but a little hard to maneuver. When the right wave came, Big Todd gave me a push, and after some frantic paddling, I got up and stood for a while until I crashed into the surf. While I was paddling out, a woman came surfing in sitting on her board with her hair all decked out in flowers, and it wasn't even wet. She looked at me and said, "Don't worry, sonny. You'll get it." I found out later that she was eighty-five years old and had been surfing since she was five years old. Surfers in Hawaii followed the waves all year round. The waves would be big on the North Shore in the winter and big on the southern shores in the summer.

It was November 7, and the presidential race between Bush and Gore was being decided in Florida, with Bush leading by only 1,600 votes. I supposed they'd have a recount. All the gang at the tennis courts were jealous of my learning to surf; all they did all day was play tennis, with no other outside interests. One day, we had a barbecue for Carol, a security officer at the airport who was going to school on the mainland for a couple of months to improve her skills. I gave her a fruit and nut basket and was allowed to hang a white ginger lei around her neck, which was a very emotional and bonding experience.

I was getting into a routine, playing tennis at sunrise, swimming two kilometers midmorning, catching a few winks on the beach, and then walking around in the afternoon checking out the town. I ran into Miki, a Japanese girl I'd met last spring who was studying English and lived in my building with another girl. I invited her over for a Christmas dinner in December.

Sears was having a holiday sale on bicycles, so I bought a mountain bike for a hundred dollars and could now branch out, covering ten miles a day.

It was November 13, and after counting and recounting, Gore finally conceded to Bush. I thought the Republicans had outsmarted the Democrats and gotten more votes than they deserved, but we'd never know.

December 10 was the twenty-eighth annual Honolulu Marathon. Some 26,000 runners from all over the world come to race, with a Kenyan man winning in two hours twenty minutes and the last person finishing in twelve hours.

One Sunday night, Miki and her roommate showed up for dinner at my condo, presenting me with an orchid and a carnation lei. They always took off their shoes before entering and bowed before giving you a hug. Well, the first thing I did was to put them to work in the kitchen, which they enjoyed immensely because they loved to help. We had a four-hour, five-course meal, starting with a cheese appetizer; the rest was cooked crab and melted butter, a Caesar salad, pasta with garlic bread and vegetables, and a dessert of ice cream and strawberries and kiwis. Well, I guess that was their first American dinner because they were writing everything down and taking pictures of everything I did. A good time was had by all. Then we bid one another Mele Kalikimaka (Merry Christmas) and Haouli Makahiki Hou (Happy New Year) and wondered if we would ever see each other again after we left Hawaii.

Loren gave me the cold shoulder at the tennis court today because I hadn't called her or come to the courts on the weekends to play; these women didn't have a sense of humor. I went swimming at Ala Moana Beach one day, but the orange flags were out, meaning box jellyfish were in the area. They came eight days after a new moon and hung around for several days. And if you got stung, the best remedy was to put vinegar or urine on the bites to stop the swelling and itching. The only problem was I hadn't figured out how to piss on myself yet.

Alice and the gang at Beachcomber Realty threw a Christmas party at their office, with great food, wine, and a harpist to put everyone in a relaxed mood, and I was invited. Alice told me that unfortunately, the owner of the condo I was staying in was coming to Hawaii. So, she found me a studio down the street at the Seashore Apartments. It worked out for the best, as the studio had just been remodeled. The kitchen was bigger and better equipped, the bed was larger, and the lanai had more privacy—all for only $650 a month. One day, I rode my bike five miles to the Waialae Golf Country Club to watch the 2001 Sony Open, which was won by Brad Faxon.

On February 12, the submarine USS *Greenville* was on a demonstration mission, and while they were making an emergency ascent, they collided with the *Ehime Maru*, a Japanese training vessel, sinking the ship and killing nine crewmen. The submarine had a bunch of dignitaries on board who distracted the crew and possibly caused the accident. Commander Waddle, the skipper, was relieved of his command and reprimanded but not court-martialed and asked to retire from the navy. He flew to Japan and personally apologized to the families but was given a cold reception. What about the women the

Japanese kept as slaves during World War II and the bombing of Pearl Harbor? Did they ever apologize?

A couple of days later, two Blackhawk helicopters collided on a training mission on the west end of Oahu, and four people were killed. Then, on April 6, an EP-3B Orion struck the tail of an A-8 Chinese fighter that crashed, and the pilot was lost. The P-3 landed at Hainan Island, and before the Chinese would release the crew, they asked for an apology. It seemed like accidents happened in groups and that the United States couldn't do anything right lately.

The thirty-eighth annual Merrie Monarch started on April 19 in Hilo, Hawaii, and lasted for four days, bringing hula contestants, both men and women, in from as far away as Texas.

One day, I called Reno Air National Guard and learned a C-130 was leaving for Hickam on April 26 and would be more than happy to bring me back to Reno. I left my bicycle with Marty, who worked at Beachcomber; cleaned the condo; and then called VIP Shuttle. They were late, though, and I wound up taking a cab to Hickam. The C-130 departed at 0830, and with some favorable tail winds, we flew eight hours nonstop, landing at Reno International just in time for a cocktail in my trailer.

CHAPTER 15

9/II

While I was planning my trip south out of Reno, at nine o'clock on the morning of September 11, 2001, under the control of Osama bin Laden, four of our commercial aircraft were hijacked. An American Airline B-767 hijacked from Logan Airport in Boston crashed into the World Trade Center, hitting the south tower and then another American Airlines B-767 hijacked from Logan Airport hit the north tower. Also, an American Airlines B-757 hijacked from Logan Airport crashed into the Pentagon. And finally, a United Airlines B-757 from Logan Airport destined to hit the White House crashed in a field in Pennsylvania. A total of twenty hijackers were involved, killing more than three thousand people and injuring thousands more.

President Bush was in Florida and immediately took to the sky to run things from Air Force One, while Vice President Cheney went to the basement of the White House with his staff. Mayor Rudolf Giuliani was very instrumental during the disaster, getting New York back on its feet. This attack was overdue, as America had become very complacent, thinking nobody could get into our country and commit such an act of terrorism.

I got tired of sitting around watching the news on television. So, as soon as the weather cleared up, I drove to Travis AFB and caught a C-5

Galaxy to Hickam AFB in Hawaii. Everywhere I went was deserted—the aircraft, the passenger terminal, lodging, Waikiki Beach, car rentals, and so on. The only tourists in Hawaii were from Europe because the Japanese were superstitious and were afraid to fly due to 9/11. I had the whole island to myself.

Alice from Beachcomber Reality found me a large studio at the Pacific Grand for $750 a month. I played tennis at Ala Moana and Kapiolani, swam at Ala Moana Beach Park, and biked around Honolulu until February 2002. Then I caught a C-5 to Richmond RAAF, Australia, via Pago Pago in American Samoa, using my retired ID card that I'd finally received since retiring from the reserves in 1982. I booked a CountryLink train to Dubbo and then a bus to Lightning Ridge in New South Wales, where I was met by my mate Gus Knee.

The town was a little quieter due to the slow Asian economy, and my caravan was still at the pistol range, less the air conditioner, stereo, and TV antenna that everyone had decided to borrow. Gus and I towed the caravan to his place in town, where I spent the next five days eating, drinking, and having a yarn with the locals.

I thought my time had come to leave this opal mining town for good. So, I signed the ownership of my caravan, Holden sedan, and Kawasaki motorcycle over to Gus and his wife, Michele, who didn't have much but had been very good to me during the past two years. After some tearful goodbyes, I retraced my steps back to Richmond RAAF, closed my Australian bank account, and caught a C-17 Globemaster back to Hickam AFB, Hawaii.

A couple days later, Monica Stanton, a tennis friend of mine, called from Reno and said her husband had committed suicide last October. She wanted me to come to Reno and comfort her. But it was still cold and snowing there, so I said I would be back sometime in May.

I stopped playing tennis at Ala Moana and Kapiolani because of a few rotten apples (tennis players) and starting playing at Diamond Head Tennis Center, as it was more relaxing.

In April, I went to the VA and had my first colonoscopy done. Both the doctor could only get three-quarters of the way up my tract because

I wasn't completely knocked out, and it hurt. The doctor took several biopsies, and they came back negative, thank God.

One day, I biked 5 miles to Pearl Harbor and played eighteen holes of golf and then to the commissary, where I saved 50 percent on groceries. I was back at my condo by cocktail time. With all the tennis, swimming, and biking I'd developed sun spots that I had a dermatologist remove. I guess the Portuguese skin my mother gave me wasn't as tough as I thought.

It was early May, and the weather in Reno was starting to get warm. So, I cleaned the condo and went to Hickam AFB to catch a flight to the mainland. Unfortunately, the C-5 that was going to Travis AFB broke down, and I wound up taking a C-130 Hercules to Las Vegas, where I met Charlie Kern, an ex U-2 pilot, and his wife on the flight. We checked into the Mandalay Bay Hotel near the airport, and I got a suite for $89 that would have cost $200 in Hawaii. The population in Las Vegas was over 1.5 million and growing at a rate of 10,000 per month. After a night of dinner, drinking, and good conversation with Charlie and his wife, I took a Southwest Airlines flight for $122 to Sacramento and then a bus to Travis AFB. I picked up my car and drove back to Reno. My neighbor and golfing partner Fred Polish had died of a heart attack three weeks earlier after I'd talked with him on the phone.

CHAPTER 16

GERMANY

Well, I called Monica. And after I'd listened to her tragic winter in Reno, we started a six-week relationship, playing golf and tennis; swimming at nude beaches at Lake Tahoe; going out to nice restaurants; and, of course, having great sex in my RV. Even though she was forty-five years old, she lacked experience in lovemaking because she had been married to one man for twenty years. I didn't mind teaching her a few things. But because she was German and very stubborn, it was very trying at times.

She started hinting about going back home to Germany with her eighteen-year-old daughter, Marie, and wanted me to come along. I told her I'd promised a tennis friend of mine I would attend his eighty-fifth birthday in Winnipeg, Manitoba, Canada.

At the end of June, I drove back to Travis AFB and caught a C-9 medivac flight to Minot AFB, North Dakota, via Boise, Idaho, and Tacoma, Washington, where I rented a Nissan Maxima and drove to Grand Forks AFB to spend the night. The next day, I drove to Winnipeg and met Joe, who found me a motel for CAN$58 (US$38) per night. For eight days, I played tennis at the Glendale Country Club in temperatures around ninety degrees and with mosquitoes as big as horseflies.

On July 1, 2002, 250 people from as far away as the Cayman Islands showed up at the club for Papa Joe's birthday. The celebration started at nine o'clock in the morning and finished at seven o'clock in the evening. I left Winnipeg and drove back to Minot AFB via Brandon, a quicker route and an easier border crossing. After spending the night at the BOQ, I caught the same C-9 back to Travis AFB, arriving after several stops en route to either pick up or drop off medical patients.

Monica went back to Germany while I was gone. So, after a summer of tennis, golf, and swimming in Reno, I drove to Fallon NAS, parked and covered my car, and then caught a C-40 (B-737) to Jacksonville NAS. The plane was deadheading back after dropping off about two hundred sailors for a two-week exercise at Fallon. The plane was empty, so I sat in the cockpit and talked with the young crew about my experiences flying in Vietnam, and they showed me all the latest equipment in the cockpit, which looked like a video game. They let me fly for a while, but when I tried to do an aileron roll, that was when I was asked to sit back in the jump seat—no sense of humor.

I told the crew I was trying to get to Germany, so they radioed ahead and found out this same plane was departing Jacksonville tomorrow morning for Naval Station Rota, Spain. I spent the night at the Jacksonville BOQ and then departed at ten o'clock in the morning for Rota via a short stop at Lajes AFB in the Azores, with only a handful of passengers on board. After seven and a half hours in the air, we approached Lajes in a lightning storm and had to abort the first attempted landing due to a fifty-knot crosswind; all I could think about was that night I'd crashed that Piper Aztec twenty years ago in Nevada and thought, *Oh no, not again.*

Fortunately, it was a quick-moving storm, and we landed safely on our second attempt. After dropping off a couple of passengers, refueling, and talking to the local Portuguese, we departed at ten o'clock that evening Azores time and arrived at NS Rota at three o'clock in the morning September 11, 2002. Since I'd left Nevada, I'd lost eight hours but gained a day. The base at Rota was under high security because of the first anniversary of the terrorist bombing in New York, and with the temperature in the midseventies, I planned to stay a few days and do some sightseeing. Unfortunately, there were no rental cars available that morning. So, I was sitting in the terminal contemplating my next move when I heard over the PA system that a C-130 was departing for Ramstein AFB, Germany, in one hour. Well, you never turn down a flight in the military because you never know when another one might come up. So, I thought, *What the hell? Let's go.*

I arrived at Ramstein, near Frankfurt just in time to check into the BOQ and make it to the officers' club for happy hour and my first taste of authentic German beer. The weather was cool, and everyone in the club was interested in where I was from because of my dark tan. Since I'd left Nevada, this trip, including food and lodging, had cost under a hundred dollars, and I'd traveled over seven thousand miles.

After a nice Italian dinner and a good bottle of wine at the club, I called a number Monica had given me. She couldn't believe I was in her country. She said the best way to get to her was by train, but I found out later that you don't just show up; you ask Germans what time they would like you to come. They're very structured and opinionated.

The next morning I took a taxi to Landstuhl train station and just caught the last train south to Munich. The ticket was $118, which included a transfer at Mannheim to an intercountry express (ICE) train that was plush and cruised at 180 miles per hour. I arrived in Munich four and a half hours later and was greeted by Monica, who seemed to be in a more serious mood than when I'd left her in Reno; these Germans were going to take a little getting used to.

Monica was born in Ginzburg, Bavaria, where her mother and brother still lived. She'd moved back to Germany because her late husband had been so far in debt he'd left her nothing but bills. At least in Germany, she has a house and a car that her mother gave her.

We departed Munich in her old Volkswagen Golf and got on the autobahn. The expressway had four lanes. The right was for trucks; the next lane was for slow vehicles; the third lane was for most traffic; and the left lane was for cars that drove 250 kilometers per hour (150 miles per hour) or faster. If you were in the left and you saw a car coming up on you, you moved over to the right. It sounds dangerous, but because it was against the law to pass on the right, everyone knew where to be, and there were very few accidents. The highways were constructed three times thicker than their US counterparts and rode very smooth, allowing BMWs, Porsches, and Mercedes to reach speeds over 350 kilometers per hour (210 miles per hour), traffic permitting. The problem was that German highways, like other European highways, were becoming very crowded; and if there was an accident at those speeds, there wasn't much left of the car or its occupants.

We arrived in Ingolstadt in about forty-five minutes, with that little Golf doing about 120 kilometers per hour (72 miles per hour). Ingolstadt was a very old town that had grown over hundreds of years without any planning, with buildings that have been constructed wherever there was space and roads that looked like a maze. When we arrived at her new apartment, I was greeted by her daughter, Marie, who I thought would be in Reno. The apartment was a one-bedroom, one-bath with a loft, and the kitchen was being remodeled. There were moving boxes stacked to the ceiling, and they were virtually living out of the bathroom. I thought about going to a hotel, but the two fräuleins talked me into staying. Little did I know I was being tested to see if I could cope with the situation.

Monica and I walked around town, drank some great Bavarian beer, had a fantastic dinner, and then went back to her apartment and had great sex in her loft. The next morning, there were people working in her kitchen, and I couldn't stand it anymore. I told Monica to pack some clothes, and we took off for the weekend. I finally got behind the wheel of that Golf and managed to get it up to 140 kilometers per hour (84 miles per hour) on the autobahn. We drove to Garmisch via Munich and then to the town of Ehrwald in Austria located at the base of Mount Zugspitze, a ski resort that's 2,962 meters (9,182 feet) high. We drove around and finally found the last room in town, which happened to be a bridle suite, egad!

I bought a bottle of champagne and we sat naked on our balcony overlooking a beautiful valley below. Then we got into another argument, as we had several times before in Reno, always after she'd had a few drinks. Well, we had sex anyway while she cried and then went out to dinner. And after that, we went back to the suite, where I introduced her to anal sex; it made her nervous at first, but she started to like it as time went by.

The next day, we took a ten-minute tram ride to the top of Zugspitze, a popular hiking and ski resort in the Alps. The weather was starting to get cool, and I was the only one up there in my shorts because I'd only brought clothes for Hawaii and didn't plan on staying in Germany that long. That afternoon, we attended a wine and cheese festival in Lermoos, where every fall, herders brought their sheep and cattle down from the mountains and decorated them for a parade through town. That night, we found a hotel in Ludwig; had a dinner of Zander, a local fish; and then danced our asses off at a nearby lounge. On the way home the next day, I got that Golf up to 160 kilometers per hour (96 miles per hour). I think I'd tune that engine up when we got back to Ingolstadt.

Claus and his sidekick finished the kitchen while we were gone, and now I was turning into a "frankfurter" helping Monica fix up the apartment and going shopping with her. I didn't know how long I'd last living with two women and one bathroom, especially when I was used to living alone. Maybe it was time to head to Hawaii.

Germany's economy was below normal, and Monica was having trouble staying employed as an athletic instructor in the public schools. She wanted her daughter to go to college here, but I thought she was homesick for her friends in Reno. I brought my tennis racquet so Monica and I played with her friends on outdoor clay courts and indoor carpet/sand courts. I swam at an outdoor pool for a few weeks until it was closed due to the drop in temperature. The indoor pool was jammed, and unlike the autobahn, people swam without lanes and would run you down.

I was having trouble with the German culture. People were very judgmental and would tell you how to conduct yourself in public. They had bicycle lanes on the sidewalk, and if you got too close to them while walking, the cyclists would yell at you. I was walking down the street one cool day in my shorts, and someone stopped me and asked if my legs were cold and said that, because everyone else was wearing long pants, maybe I should do the same. Then at a party one night with Monica, a woman came up to me and said I had a "roving eye" and shouldn't be looking at the other women.

The Germans were also very ecologically conscious with fuel-efficient cars, low cost heating, recycling everything in sight, and keeping their cities and country as clean as possible. The problem was 88 million people were living in a country the size of Texas, and they were running out of space. Parking was at a premium in town, and if you were on the autobahn during rush hour, you could be going two hundred kilometers per hour and then come to a complete stop. Computer-generated signs above the autobahn let you know what the traffic was like ahead and was kept current twenty-four hours a day.

The people wouldn't speak English, even though they could but expected you to speak German. When I first arrived in this country, I thought I would see blond, fair-skinned Germans. But they were only in the north. In Bavaria the people were dark-haired with ruddy skin, and I believe it's because they're so close to those Italian and Spanish people.

One weekend, I took Monica and Marie to Munich for shopping. Because it was getting so cold I wound up buying some Levi's, a Bavarian shirt, a leather jacket, and some suede loafers. After a drink at Famous Schumanns, we drove through heavy rain to the town of Starnberg for the night and then to Füssen to tour Neuschwanstein Castle, built in 1869 by King Ludwig II. The castle was where the king's friend Richard Wagner composed his music.

We spent the night in a beautiful hotel and spa, where everyone ran around naked. Marie said it was the first time she could remember anyone treating her and her mother like queens. On the way home, I finally got that little Golf up to 180 kilometers per hour (108 miles per hour)—must have been the tune-up I'd given it the previous week.

One night while Monica was working late, Marie and I got drunk together, and she opened up, telling me that her mother was an alcoholic and that Monica's mother was also an alcoholic. When they'd lived in Reno, Monica would hide bottles of vodka all over the house so nobody would know when she was drinking. That explained the arguments she would get me into after a few glasses of wine and the trouble she had with orgasms at night but not during the day. The way Marie would put away beer, I supposed she would turn out just like her mother.

One day, Marie got a call from a brew master friend of hers from

Reno who was coming over to study German brewing. Well, we all dressed up Bavarian style, including my lederhosen and then drove to Munich International to pick up Marie's friend. From there, we headed to the famous Octoberfest in Munich. It was a crazy day, with the fest lasting two weeks and consisting of about a half dozen tents with a capacity of two thousand people in each, eating, drinking, and dancing on the tables to nonstop Bavarian bands. There was a grassy knoll nearby that people would stagger up to and pass out. When they woke up, they would go back to the tents and start drinking all over again. Unfortunately, I was the designated driver, so all I could do was watch everyone make fools of each other. September was the month of wine fests, and October was for beer fests; I wondered when these people worked.

A week later, Marie decided to go back to Reno. So, we threw her a party the night before and barely got up to drive her to the airport.

Well, I thought things would calm down after Marie left, but Monica was becoming very moody and demanding and too domesticated for me. It was the middle of October, cold and rainy. I'd installed a washer and dryer, built cabinets, put up track lighting, and painted her apartment. Plus, the sex wasn't good anymore, as Monica went out with her friends at night and got drunk.

One night, she decided we should get married and have a child, which was enough to scare the hell out of me. So, I bought a train ticket back to Landstuhl and told her I would call her when I arrived in Hawaii. Well, it was like a scene in a Humphrey Bogart movie. We were standing on the train platform in the cold rain holding each other, and she looked up into my eyes and thought, *I am never going to see this guy again.*

Well, she was right. I never looked back. And while speeding along in the train at two hundred kilometers per hour sipping a glass of Bordeaux, I felt a huge weight lifted from my shoulders. I caught a C-5 Galaxy out of Ramstein AFB to Dover AFB, Delaware, and met an army colonel who had been married to a German for thirty-five years. He laughed at what I had just gone through and said the women are very demanding. And you don't tell them what to do; you ask them what to do. He thought his wife would have changed after all those years, but she was as stubborn as the day they'd met, and I was lucky to get out alive.

I left Dover the next morning on another C-5 to Travis AFB, but when we landed, two hundred people were in the passenger terminal waiting for a flight to Hawaii. I talked with one of the passengers, who said flights had been cancelled all week, causing the backup. There was no lodging, so I found a motel off base, and the next morning, I bought a ticket to Honolulu from Sun Trips for $229, leaving Oakland International the next morning. I guess I could afford it, being that the entire flight to Germany and back had been free.

While I was waiting for ground transportation that night to Oakland, a C-5 landed unannounced with fifty vacant seats. Since there were only a handful of us in the terminal, I got on the flight and figured I would use my Sun Trips ticket at a later date. I arrived at Hickam AFB at three o'clock in the morning and then rested in the terminal until nine o'clock, when I picked up a car from Enterprise car rental. I drove to the Subase BOQ for a room and then took a swim, had dinner, and crashed for ten hours due to the jet lag from Germany. I played tennis the next day at Diamond Head and then went to see Alice at Beachcomber Realty, but she didn't have any condos for rent because she thought I was still in Germany. She finally put me in the Ilikai for a month and then the Pavilion for a month at $1,100 each and would move me as soon as something cheaper came up.

Representative Linda Lingle, a Republican was elected governor of Hawaii on November 5, 2002, replacing Democratic Cayetano, who had been cheating Hawaii out of millions of dollars over the years. The Ala Wai Canal was finally dredged after twenty years; during one dredge, they pulled up a twenty-pound shrimp. I wondered what else is living down there.

I stayed in the Pavilion until January 1, 2003, and then rented a studio condo from Ron Fredericks at the Holliday Village near Ala Moana Shopping Center for $775 a month. The place was a little dirty, so I told Ron, if he supplied the tools and materials, I would fix it up. The weather in Reno was nasty, with twenty-foot snowdrifts, avalanches at Mt. Rose and eighty-mile-per-hour winds. I thought it was time I move to Hawaii permanently.

I had all my mail forwarded to the Holliday Village from Reno and changed my cell phone to a Hawaii number. I started working on the condo, painting the ceiling, tiling the kitchen and bathroom, replacing the toilet, fixing the refrigerator, repairing the sink, adding a box spring to the bed after fixing the frame, and putting a new screen on the sliding door. After all that work, all Ron did was take me to dinner and a movie, never offering to give me a break on the rent; some people only know how to take and not give.

Koichi, a tennis friend of mine, invited me to a free ukulele lesson at the Royal Hawaiian one day. It was difficult at first, but eventually, I got the hang of it and bought my own ukulele for thirty dollars with a case. I'd learned a half a dozen songs with the group, which consisted of about twenty other players, the Hukilau being my favorite. Now my routine was tennis three times a week, a two-kilometer swim in the ocean three times a week, golf twice a week, and ukulele lessons twice a week. What a great year around life.

On January 31, 2003, the space shuttle *Columbia* was returning from the space station but broke up at two hundred thousand feet during reentry from a damaged leading edge wing that occurred during liftoff. The pieces were scattered over east Texas, leaving no survivors. The accident was due to the lack of funding for NASA; consequently, the agency's quality control program had gone to hell. George Bush was preoccupied with Iraq and Saddam Hussein and his weapons of mass destruction. So, I figured, one day, we were going to war with him.

CHAPTER 17

MY MOVE TO HAWAII

It was March 1, and things were finally starting to thaw out in Reno. So, I caught a military-contracted DC-8 from Hickam to Travis with stewardesses and hot meals and then took a city bus to Suisun, where I got a Greyhound Bus to Reno because my car was in Fallon, Nevada. The next day, Art, my tennis and golf buddy, and I went to Fallon to pick up my Ranchero. But the wind had blown the cover off during the winter, and there was sand everywhere including in the engine; that was Nevada for you.

One morning, I woke up to a foot of snow and said, "That's it. I'm selling everything and moving to Hawaii." I boxed up my personal effects and shipped them via UPS to Beachcomber Reality in Honolulu for two dollars a pound.

It was March 19, 2003, and George Bush was tired of listening to Saddam's lies, so he put a two thousand-pound bunker buster bomb into one of Saddam's buildings, killing a couple of top aids and wounding Saddam. Operation Iraqi Freedom had begun, and within three weeks, we had control of Bagdad.

While I was waiting for someone to buy my trailer and car, I played tennis and golf with Art in Reno. One day, I held a garage sale, and what I couldn't sell, I gave away. Somebody finally bought my trailer, but I had to finance it for a year. The Ranchero wouldn't sell because I was asking too much. I guess I didn't want to get rid of that classic. I called Matson Lines, and for $900, they would ship my car from Oakland to Honolulu; it would take about a week.

I drove down to Travis AFB for a few days, playing golf and staying in a suite with a kitchen for sixteen dollars a night. I drove to Matson Lines in Oakland and dropped off my car and then took a taxi to a Motel Six near the airport, where I had to pay sixty dollars a night for a little room in a high-crime neighborhood. I finally arrived at the Oakland airport for my flight with the Sun Trips ticket I'd bought last year. They put me on standby. And would you believe it? I got the last seat on a sold-out flight.

My car arrived at Matson on Sand Island in Honolulu after five days at sea. Now, I had to find a place to park it because my condo parking lot was full, causing me to go to a covered parking garage two blocks away for forty-five dollars a month until a space became available at my condo. I went to the DMV and got my Hawaiian driver's license, which entitled me to Kamaaina rates (75 percent less than nonresidents). Cars in Hawaii required a safety check every year that cost twenty dollars, and a registration fee, determined by the weight at three cents a pound. The Ranchero weighed 4,050 pounds.

I was having trouble adjusting to the driving habits on the island; it seemed everyone was fighting for what little space there was on the highways—unlike Nevada, with all that open space. There were over a million cars on Oahu, and during rush hour in and out of Honolulu, the freeways were at a standstill. The only time I drove was when I played golf at the Klipper Course at Kaneohe on the windward side of the island or went to the VA at Tripler Army Hospital. The rest of the time, I rode my bicycle. The boxes of my personal effects had arrived, but they looked like they'd gone to Iraq first. Next time, I'd remember to write fragile on everything.

Well, I turned sixty-two this year. And on July 1, my first social security check arrived in my bank account, something I'd completely forgotten about. With that, my military retirement pay, and the loans coming in from Nevada, Hawaii wouldn't be as expensive as I'd thought.

I couldn't believe how much my body had gotten out of shape during the six weeks I'd been in Reno; it was good to get back into my exercise routine. My body wasn't the only thing that needed to be tuned; so did my mind. So, I enrolled in an astronomy course at the University of Hawaii. But when I arrived for the first class, it was standing room only. I bought the book and decided to study the course on my own. I just wouldn't be able to observe the stars with the class.

I spent most of the summer working on the condo and decided it was time I bought one for myself. So, Ron, who was a realtor, and I went all around the island looking at studios and one-bedroom apartments priced around $100,000. I wanted a little grass shack near the beach, but the land was over $500,000, with the shack thrown in for free. Then in November 2003, a unit in my building came up for sale. But there were five offers. I was the sixth and thought I wouldn't have a chance. Can you believe it? All the offers fell through because nobody had the down payment, and I wound up paying $105,000 for a studio on the eighth floor with a makai (ocean), skyline, and mauka (mountain) view. The building, which was completely round, was constructed in 1964. So, the studio was pretty much original but clean.

The first thing I did was to tear up the old carpet and linoleum and rip out the old kitchen countertop. Then I painted the ceiling, walls, and kitchen cabinets. I laid ceramic tile in the entranceway, bathroom, and kitchen and a strip along the lanai window so the new carpet wouldn't get wet or fade. Then I put in a new countertop, florescent light, faucet, and garbage disposal. I also bought a couple of cabinet kits from Home Depot and a piece of three-quarter-inch plywood and built a counter (bar) between the kitchen and living room. Then I tiled everything in the kitchen, including the counter. I was very fortunate because Ron loaned me all the tools, including a tile cutter. Plus, living in the same building made it very convenient to work. After the new carpet was put in, I installed an air conditioner and a sliding drape that blocked out the afternoon sun.

My last and most difficult project was installing a twelve-volt track lighting system on the ceiling that required running wires through the inner walls. While I was drilling holes in the concrete ceiling, I put too much pressure on my lower back and forced meniscus fluid out between two lower vertebrae. The doctor said it would take about six weeks of rest, taking muscle relaxing pills and ibuprofen, before the fluid would return, with no tennis, no golf, no swimming, and no bike riding. I was glad he didn't opt for surgery because a tennis friend of mine had a similar problem, and the doctor had cut the wrong nerve. Now, he walked around with a waste bag tied to his hip because he lost control of his intestinal tract.

Ron came by my condo and said it was the best-looking unit in the building and wanted to sell it for $160,000. But then where would I go? Prices were starting to rise, and the availability of housing was becoming scarce.

The following month, word got out that I was a handyman. So, I renovated a unit in the building managed by Alice Lombardi of Beachcomber Realty in exchange for ten days and nights at a condo in Waikiki, which I let Phil Hosking, my financial advisor from Reno, use. I also renovated a unit for Shirley Raffa, who lived in our building, a $1,500 job I only charged her $800 for because I'm such a nice guy— yeah, right!

The day after Thanksgiving, I was driving west on the H-1 Freeway to Tripler Hospital at fifty miles per hour, when all of a sudden, everyone came to a full stop, and I rear-ended a Honda. Nobody was hurt, so we exchanged names and insurance companies and were on our way. The body shop quoted $2,700 to replace my right front fender and parking light. So, the insurance company totaled my car and sent me the blue book value of $1,500, less $100 because I bought the car back from them.

I was used to living on the mainland, where wrecking yards were full of Rancheros. In Hawaii it was a different story. Consequently, it took me four months and $400 to find a fender and light from San Diego, California. The Dent Doctors in Honolulu repaired the car for $500, and I still had $500 left over.

I thought about selling that car, but with the methamphetamine (ICE) epidemic here, people were stealing new cars, stripping them, and shipping the parts back to the mainland. I had an old bike I rode for a few years that I never locked, and nobody would bother it. But when I bought a new Schwinn with all the shock absorbers and gears, it lasted a month. One night in Waikiki, a bike thief cut the lock and stole the damn thing. I bought a cheaper bike with a stronger lock but never took it out at night anymore.

Well, it was the beginning of 2004, and the war in Iraq was escalating, to the point that we'd lost four hundred soldiers to sniper fire, suicide bombers, and roadside explosive devices, but we'd killed or captured 80 percent of Saddam's henchmen. The media was making a big deal out of losing thirty to forty of our troops every month. But during the Vietnam War, we lost five hundred men a month for ten years, and nobody gave a damn. I thought it was just a matter of time before we captured or killed Saddam Hussein; without his henchmen, he was, like most leaders, a mere coward.

The hurricane season in 2004 had been the worst we'd seen in over a century, with Florida getting hit four times, killing hundreds and leaving thousands homeless. I was glad I'd moved to the Hawaiian Islands, which were rarely hit by hurricanes because they're such a small target in such a large ocean. The only time the islands were at risk was during El Niño, which happened about every seven years, causing a three hundred-mile diameter body of warm ocean water that moved north from South America, increasing the amount of hurricanes on the Pacific coast. Another problem would be a tsunami caused by earthquakes in the Pacific Ocean.

Ronald Reagan, our fortieth president, died on June 5, 2004, from complications of Alzheimer's disease; he was ninety-three years old.

Jerry Ling, a local handyman, had helped me with some of my electrical and plumbing problems and stopped by once in a while for a couple of beers. He said someone gave him a beer-making kit about five years ago, but it was still sitting in his garage. So, I asked him to bring it over, and I would give it a try. By trial and error and a little help from the Hawaiian Homebrew Store, I achieved my aim. It took me about six months, but I finally produced a dark porter that tasted as good as the Brew Moon Brewery here in Honolulu and a lot cheaper—fifty cents compared to four dollars a pint.

The process of making beer starts with buying the malt that comes either in a pale wheat or dark, syrupy mixture. It's then boiled in water for an hour with either English, German, or Western hops for taste. The malt can also be mixed to make dark wheat, porter, stout, and so on, and flavors can be added, such as cherry, raspberry, passion fruit, guava, and the like. After the malt and hops (wort) cool down, it's added to a sterile gallon of water, shaken, and put in the refrigerator until it cools down to seventy degrees. A hydrometer is used to check liquid density, and then yeast is added to start the fermentation process, which takes six to ten days keeping the liquid between seventy and eighty degrees. The hydrometer is used again to determine alcohol level, usually 6 percent to 10 percent depending on the amount of sugar in the fruit used. The beer is now ready for bottling by adding corn sugar that has been boiled in water. This will create the carbonation. I used twenty-two ounce bottles that I sealed with a bottle capper and stored for a minimum of ten days at seventy-five degrees. The longer you wait, the smoother it gets. Some beer makers wait up to a year, but I drink it as soon as possible; life is too short.

They finally captured Saddam, who was hiding in a hole on a ranch outside Tikrit but wouldn't put up a fight. So, we had to take him alive. He and his cronies would go to trial next year with a good possibility of being executed.

Now that I was finished with my condo, it was time to start fixing up the Ranchero. I went to the Hickam AFB auto shop and started removing all the chrome, trim, bumpers, grill, headlights, and so on. A young local boy who worked in the parts room asked if I was going to do the body work and paint it myself, and I said, "Make me an offer."

He was just graduating from Honolulu City College in the auto shop department and said he would do my car for $1,200—a job that would have cost me $4,000 anyplace in town. Well, it took a month, and the paint job turned out great, with gold flakes in the metallic brown. Then I took the Ranchero to Cosmic and had a picture of an F-4 airbrushed on the fiberglass lid that you couldn't see unless you looked real close. I had the interior redone, and I was told the car was worth around $12,000. But I didn't think I'd ever sell it.

When I drove around the island, I'd get a lot of compliments on my car, especially from the old local boys. The car was running better than it ever had, even though there were over 250,000 miles on the engine. I found a covered parking stall next to my building for $85 a month, with my condo on the eighth floor and my car on the fourth floor. I figured I was very safe from a tsunami.

The Elite Electronics stereo installation place, a VIP prostitution parlor, and an illegal gambling hall in the Samsung Plaza below my lanai were keeping me awake twenty-four hours a day. So, I went to the neighborhood board meeting to complain. The next thing I knew, I was elected to the board. We met once a month with police, fire, senators, governor's and mayor's representatives' and developers attending to keep us abreast of the goings-on in the Ala Moana / Kakaako district. I figured maybe someday we'd be able to clean up all the bars and strip clubs that had been here for such a long time, especially with five new high-rises being built that would create 1,500 units in the area.

Financially, I was doing pretty well. My income averaged $4,000 a month, and my total expenditures—including mortgage, golf, food, gas, and such—were $1,500, leaving me with about $2,500 a month to put in the bank or invest. I didn't have any medical or dental expenses because I used the military and Veterans Administration. I didn't think anyone could live as well and as cheaply as I did.

On December 27, 2005, Dr. Dow, a neurologist from the VA, took six biopsies from my prostate and said 80 percent looked good. But he sent one of the biopsies to Walter Reed Hospital in Washington, DC, for a second opinion and should get results in a few weeks. In the meantime, I couldn't exercise, drink liquor, or have sex for two weeks. Well, hell, I'd just as soon die now. But the doctor told me to hang in there. Finally, the tests came back, and I was good as new. So, I could get back to my regular exercise routine.

Chikara Yanagiya (Liki), a tennis partner of mine, had introduced me to a friend of his last year. Eriko Dmitrovsky lived in Paris and also had an apartment in Hong Kong and Hawaii and came here twice a year. The first thing she said when she came back to Hawaii and called me was that her stereo was broken. Unfortunately, it was a twelve-year-old Yamaha, and no parts were available anymore. I invited her over to my apartment for a six-course dinner and wine one night. Afterward, she jumped on my bed and tore off her clothes. She was a forty-nine-year-old Japanese woman who'd been married for ten years to a Russian engineer who died of cancer. I thought she hadn't had much sex since then because she had ten orgasms that night during a twelve-hour sex marathon.

I gave her amplifier to Mac Mcglaughlin, an electronics wizard who lived in my condo and said he'd try and fix it. Eriko invited Mac and his wife, Libba; Liki and me; and Eriko's friend Jean for dinner one night at her two-bedroom apartment at the Admiral Thomas Condos (which was worth $900,000, with a maintenance fee of $1,100 a month). After everyone left, Eriko and I had sex all night, a marathon during which she had twenty more orgasms. A week later, I brought her over to my apartment, where she had ten orgasms. A few days later, I went to her place for the night, and she had ten more orgasms.

The only problem was, every time I saw her, she seemed to have something broken in her apartment and wanted me to fix it. She was also a smoker and, it seemed to me, an alcoholic, as she was very demanding. It was driving me away, kind of like the fräulein from Ingolstadt. I didn't think we were getting along because she was using me. When I tried to end the relationship, she told me she was from royalty and was the eldest sister of five in Japan. I suppose that was just a ploy to keep me from trying to break off our relationship. She said she had been very athletic when she was younger but was out of shape now and lived in the past because of the death of her husband. I took her to the Seabreeze for dinner one night at Hickam AFB, but all she did was show her attraction to young babies in the restaurant, trying to convince me she could be a good mother.

The next night she invited me for leftovers from her St. Patrick's Day party that I hadn't been invited to. After another argument, I finally said goodbye while she was standing at the dinner table pouring a glass of wine with the dinner she'd prepared. The next day, I dropped off that broken Yamaha at her condo and washed my hands of her for good. We just didn't get along because she had no sense of humor.

On February 20, 2006, there were low pressures to the south. So, it started raining and continued for forty days and forty nights, flooding all the islands and causing several deaths on Kauai because of a reservoir that gave way. And would you believe this rain stopped as soon as I quit seeing Eriko?

The worst problem of the storm was on March 28, when a sewer main in Waikiki that was supposed to have been replaced seven years ago broke, and the city pumped 50 million gallons of raw sewage into the Ala Wai Canal for two days while they temporarily repaired the main. They polluted Ala Moana Beach, Waikiki Beach, and Magic Island waters. And when a thirty-four-year-old mortgage broker fell off a boat in the Ala Wai Harbor, he was hospitalized with feces bacteria that attacked his vital organs through an open wound. He died several days later. A female surfer who cut her buttocks on some coral also got sick with four types of bacterial infections and was still in the hospital. Also, a German man who'd been living here for twelve years, was walking along Waikiki Beach with a metal detector and cut his foot. The next day, his leg swelled up, and the doctors were thinking about amputation. Most of the beaches around the island were closed because of sewage spills, and Honolulu was so worried about keeping the tourists that some beaches didn't have any signs warning the public of the problem. A friend of mine flew in from the mainland and said he saw brown water all around the island and extending a mile out to sea. This island was spending too much money building new high-rises but wasn't updating the sewage system, which had been slated for repairs in 1997. The powers that be needed to stop the growth before it got out of hand.

The median price of a house on Oahu was over $600,000, and a condo averaged over $300,000, which was causing more people to become homeless. Families with an annual income of $30,000 were living in tents on the beaches and parks. A new high-rise in downtown Honolulu sold one-bedroom units last month for $535,000 and penthouses for $1.2 million. My studio that I'd paid $100,000 for two years ago was worth $250,000 today. The local Hawaiians were selling their old houses for $800,000 and moving in together. There was a fire in Honolulu the other day that destroyed a two-bedroom house from which seventeen people were evacuated. The island was becoming very dangerous every day, especially for the tourists who left valuables in their cars while enjoying the scenery. The local Hawaiians hung out in parking lots around the island beaches, and when they saw you out taking pictures, they broke into your car and were gone within minutes, maybe even with your car.

I'd been swimming at Ala Moana Beach Park for about eight years, and each time I went for my one-hour swim, I left a small backpack on the beach, usually near other sunbathers. The other day when I returned, I discovered that someone, probably a homeless person, had gone through every zippered pocket and taken anything of value. It was a good thing I didn't leave any credit cards or identification. Now, most of us swimmers left our gear next to the lifeguard station. At least it wasn't as bad as Waikiki, where they have plainclothes police officers patrolled the beaches watching the thieves.

When I golfed at Marine Corp Base in Kaneohe or any other military base, it was like another part of the world, where everyone trusted one another. I bike about 5 miles to NAS Pearl Harbor a couple times a week along a bike path under the H-1 Freeway, where the homeless people hung out, and I was afraid that, one day, I was going to get mugged.

It was June 8, 2006, and our special task forces finally located Abu Musab al-Zarqawi, al-Qaida's leader in Iraq, who led a bloody campaign of suicide bombings and kidnappings. An F-16 struck a safe house that was a result of intelligence reports provided to Iraqi security forces by residents in Diyala, thirty miles northeast of Bagdad. We were still looking for Osama bin Laden, who was believed to be holed up in a cave in Tora Bora, Afghanistan. I guessed it was just a matter of time before we developed more sophisticated equipment that would locate him. Saddam Hussein had gone on a hunger strike, protesting his trial. Why didn't we just let him kill himself? This war was dragging on longer than anyone expected. Besides the insurgents attacking the Iraqis, the Shia were now attacking the Sunni. These people had hated one another longer than we thought.

The United States needed to focus more on alternate energy, such as solar, wind, hydroelectric, ethanol, hydrogen, and ocean wave motion power, and stop using oil, which would dry up imports from other countries that relied so heavily on us. We also needed to reduce our use of cocaine, which was financing terrorists around the world, especially in Afghanistan.

Around July 10, 2006, terrorists from Lebanon kidnapped two Israeli soldiers, and a war finally broke out, with Israel sending air strikes to Hezbollah and Hezbollah firing unguided rockets into Israel, killing innocent women and children. Iran and Syria were supplying Hezbollah with the rockets, and we were supplying Israel with bombs. And who knew how long this war would continue?

Mac, a retired Navy pilot who was in poor health due to exposure to Agent Orange in Vietnam, lived in the building with his wife, Libba. He didn't have much and was just getting by. So, once a week, I took them out to dinner or invited them down to my condo for a meal and drinks and good conversation. Toward the end of July, Mac's landlord said he was selling the condo and asked them to move out. But because of Mac's health, he was admitted to the hospital as a result of the mental and physical stress from moving. He died a week later of internal bleeding.

Hawaii had added 10 percent ethanol to our gas. So, I had all the rubber fuel hoses in my car replaced with high-pressure hoses and also added Bio Performance tablets to the fuel to reduce contamination and improve gas mileage.

Sunday morning at 7:00 a.m., October 15, 2006, the Big Island of Hawaii was hit with a 6.7 earthquake situated six miles north of the island at a depth of thirteen miles, which was deep enough to prevent a tsunami. Because of some old sensor switches Hawaiian Electric Company had, transformers started shutting down on Oahu, cutting off power to the entire island for fourteen hours. I wished I lived in a house in the country because you were at the mercy of a condominium with no power or water. I lived on the eighth floor, so the lack of elevator didn't bother me—unlike older residents on the twentieth floor.

The locals on the island took everything in stride, firing up their BBQs and inviting the neighbors over for a party. There was no looting at the stores, and few people were in their cars, leaving the roads open. I invited Lisa, my Korean neighbor, over, and we spent the day together, listening to a local radio station for updates and cooking a nice meal. I had a gas stove, and if I kept the refrigerator closed, the food would last most of the day.

Phil Hosking came to Maui for two weeks, so I flew to Kapalua on Go Airlines for twenty-nine dollars and spent a week with him. He had rented a condo in Kihei that was on the beach. We spent most of the time driving around the island looking at houses and condos that were priced a little less than those on Oahu because of a housing slump. The only problem for me was that I depended on the military for medical, dental, optical, commissary, and so on, and Maui had nothing.

One day, we went to Kapalua, where the Mercedes Open, the first PGA tournament of the year, took place. Most of the island's construction was on that side of the island, with a lot of golfers owning condos there. We also took a ferry over to Molaka'i for a day and drove around the island that was still the same after a hundred years or more and still housed people with leprosy. The population was six thousand, with few roads and beaches and not much to do. But I could say I'd been there. On the way back to Maui that afternoon, we ran into a storm and hit twenty-foot waves that caused most of the passengers on the ferry to become seasick. Can you believe that this was the first time I'd been off Oahu since I'd moved here three years ago? I guess when you live in paradise, there's no place else you want to go.

I caught a flight back to Honolulu and then the Bus to Hickam AFB, where I'd left my car at the passenger terminal for free.

Well, New Year's Eve was a little quieter this time. I figured, one year, fireworks would be outlawed for individuals, letting the professionals put on the shows. The year was very costly to our troops in Iraq, where over three thousand had been killed and no end in sight. Saddam Hussein was finally executed at the end of 2006 by hanging, along with his half brothers. Gerald Ford, our thirty-eighth president, who was the oldest living president, died at the age of ninety-three.

I volunteered for the Sony Open golf tournament in Waialae on January 11, 2007, working with the ShotLink that measures the distance the ball travels off the tee. I also volunteered with the Senior PGA Championship at Turtle Bay on January 25, the SBS Women Tournament in Turtle Bay on February 13, and the Fields Women Tournament in Ko Olina on February 21. The crowds that came to these tournaments were very laid-back, unlike those on the mainland, which made the players friendlier.

I received a letter from Melanie, one of my nieces, who found out where I lived from the internet. I guess my life wasn't very private anymore. On July 2, a Superferry arrived from the mainland; it was 380 feet long, cruised at thirty-five knots, and carried 850 passengers plus 280 cars. It would ferry people to Kauai and Maui, with a second ferry due the beginning of 2009 that would go to the Big Island.

The transmission in the Ranchero finally gave out after fifteen years, so I had it rebuild. And it shifts like a brand-new car. But the cost was $1,400, still cheaper than a new car. The Superferry finally sailed but was met at Kauai by protesters and told not to return so it went to Maui with less resistance and was allowed to enter. The Superferry sailed once a day for thirty-nine dollars per person and fifty dollars per car as an introductory promotion until 2008.

The Feds and HPD finally raided the gambling room in the Samsung Plaza outside my lanai. They arrested a Korean man and his wife and found $7 million in property, stocks, and cash the couple had amassed over a year. They were convicted and put away for a while, so it was a little quieter in the neighborhood at nights.

I took a spill on my bike one day when the front tire blew out, causing me to bruise my ribs and skin myself up. I walked my bike for a mile to the bike shop and had two new tires and tubes put on for eighty dollars; it seems that, when you bought a new bike, it had cheap tires and tubes installed. I was laid up for a couple of weeks, no tennis, golf, or swimming. I finally broke my recliner, so I went to Home World and found an $800 plush recliner for $500—what a difference from that small recliner I had before.

I stopped by Plywood of Hawaii and found an oak veneer four-by-eight, precut panel that made two cabinet doors for $50—saved $100. I called the IRS about my refund for 2006, but I opened a can of worms. They started looking into 2005 and sent me a tax bill for $2,600 because I hadn't reported my loan interests. Well, I'd been doing it for ten years. So, I sent them a check immediately, hoping they wouldn't go back any further.

One night, I got up out of bed and fainted, falling down and breaking a stool, I think I should get up a little slower from now on. On August 7, 2007, Barry Bonds of the San Francisco Giants broke Hank Aaron's record by hitting 756 home runs but may get indicted for steroid use. The US Air Force F-16 Thunderbirds put on an air show over Magic Island on September 13, 2007, with the first woman pilot. But they're a lot more conservative than the Navy Blue Angles.

I'd been having electrical problems in the Ranchero lately, with my battery always going dead. So, I had a buzzer installed in case I left my lights on. I finally found the original thirty-year-old voltage regulator was not charging the battery. I replaced it for thirteen dollars—not bad for an old car. I also drove over the Pali Highway and had to have my brakes replaced after fifteen thousand miles for $600.

I couldn't seem to hit my golf irons anymore. So, I bought three TaylorMade rescue clubs and took the number three through the number five irons out of my bag, and my golf score went down. I play once a week at the Klipper Course at the Marine Corps Base in Kaneohe for sixteen dollars a round with Tony, a retired marine who was a PGA player/instructor. The rest of the time, I went to public courses like Ted Makalena, Pali, Ala Wai, West Lochs, and Ewa Village for a seven-dollar senior walking rate. And they said it was expensive to live in Hawaii. I also played tennis twice a week at Diamond Head Tennis Center and swam two kilometers three times a week at Ala Moana Beach Park.

Honolulu continued to grow with condominiums; plus, the traffic was getting worse. Mayor Mufi Hannemann was trying to put in a light rail system from the west side of the island to downtown Honolulu to reduce freeway traffic; it took commuters two hours to drive each way. But it was going to cost about $3 billion. I decided that, when the second Superferry came, I might take my car to the Big Island and look around, as housing was a lot cheaper, it was quieter, and there was a lot more room.

One day, I sent a letter to Elite Electronics in the Samsung telling them, if their stereo installer didn't turn down the noise, I would trash his pickup. Well, a week later I got a call from the prosecutors' office of the HPD because Elite Electronics filed a complaint. So, I went down there and told the prosecutor that, if the police didn't do anything about the continuous noise, I would. All he could say was, "I sympathize with you."

I tried to meet Chief of Police Boise Carrera, but he referred me to one of his subordinates, and I never got anywhere. The HPD was different from police forces on the mainland. Most of their employees were local Hawaiians, and they seemed to take care of their own—be that drug dealers, thieves, domestic violence perpetrators, carjackers, those participating in prostitution or strip bars, and on and on. They got paid "under the table" and looked the other way. Last year, several officers were caught dealing drugs, but you never heard what happened to them. So, the corruption continued.

Kainoa Gillette, our resident manager, finally got sixty signatures on a petition that I took to the liquor commission to have the noise stopped at Club Tsunami, and it worked.

The year of 2007 was running down, with more than four thousand troops killed in Iraq and no end in sight. Senator John McCain won the republican candidacy for president, and Hillary Clinton and Barak Obama were fighting it out for the Democratic spot; it was very close. We had a normal winter rainy season, but I thought we were in for a drought next year. And because of El Niño, there was a chance of more hurricanes.

The New Year's celebration was very quiet again, except for the locals setting off illegal aerial fireworks in town. I caught a couple of them near our condo and guarded the evidence until the HPD arrived. But they did nothing, even though I gave them a description and license plate number of the vehicle involved.

I was still giving platelets at the blood center at Tripler Army Hospital, receiving a plaque every year because I was the second top donor in the military in Hawaii. There was a premature baby at Triple that was no bigger than the palm of my hand, and I was keeping it alive until it finally grew to a normal sized baby; it was a great feeling. Every year, I bought dolls and games for the kids at Kakaako Outreach Center Homeless Shelter for Christmas; it was the least I could do.

The 2008 Sony Open was at Waialae January 9 through 13. I volunteered with the ShotLink group measuring the length of drives on the fairway and putts on the green. K. J. Choi won the tournament. I then volunteered for the senior championship at Turtle Bay from January 25 through 27, with Jerry Pate winning that tournament. I went back to Turtle Bay for the SBS LPGA tournament from February 13 through 17. Anikka Sorenstam won and had a picture taken with Natalie Gulbis on the signature seventeenth hole, which she enlarged and signed. The last tournament was the Fields Open at Ko Olina, from February 21 through 23, with Paula Creamer winning. I wasn't sure if the championship or Fields Open would be held here next year, as they couldn't get anyone to sponsor the tournament; we shall see.

Lisa, my Korean neighbor, was moving back to Seoul. So, I invited her over for dinner one night, and we finally had sex after knowing each other for four years. Before she left, she told me to buy a two-bedroom condo so she would have a place to stay when she returned. These Koreans were very demanding people, unlike the more courteous Japanese women.

Phil Hosking had a $100,000 loan at 12 percent, giving me $1,200 a month income, so I emptied my bank account, which I hoped was the right thing to do. Because of Go Airlines competing in Hawaii, Aloha Airline filed for bankruptcy; now the prices would start going up again. Mike Adams, my next door neighbor, was putting in new kitchen cabinets that would cost him about $4,000. So, I went to Lowes in Waipahu and ordered just the doors for a quarter of the cost. Laurie, who took my order, was a cute surfer on the North Coast and wanted to get together and take me snorkeling. But we never made contact.

My two nieces from the mainland, Melannie and Delores, found my address on the internet. it was hard to hide out in this world anymore. If they could find me, why couldn't we find Osama bin Laden?

I went to Hickam AFB Dental, but they were too busy for walk-ins. So I went to MCBH for a checkup, and the oral hygienist recommended

I see a periodontal dentist. I went to Dr. Iha in the Pan Am Building near my condo, and he told me I needed cleaning under my gums that would cost $4,000. I signed up with Delta Dental, a part of Tri Care. They would cover $3,000 with my monthly premium of $43. I had the right side of my mouth done first. It took two hours in the chair and a month of recovery. But it was a one-time operation, thank god. I guess it was hereditary. My father had neglected his gums and lost his lower front teeth. Some people have it done at forty years of age, and others never have a problem.

Lowes finally called, so I picked up my cabinet doors and drawers and my kitchen looks like new for only a $1,000—what a deal. The only thing left to do was install a glass shower door. But because of the pie-shaped condo, it had to be custom-made, and I was having trouble finding a specialist.

It was August 7, 2008, and the XXIX Summer Olympics started in Beijing with the United States winning the most medals but China winning the most gold. The Chinese women's gymnastics group was protested by Olympic authorities because none of them had any birth certificates, and you knew they were underage. China, with a population of 2 billion, had to stop all factories and automobiles because of the smog that would hurt outside sports competition during the Olympics. China has also been caught exporting dog food, baby formula, cookies, and more with pesticides found in the product that had killed animals in the United States and babies in China. Apparently, this has been going on for a long time but had just been discovered.

Mortgage companies had been loaning money on houses with low or no down payment for the last two years, and it was finally back firing. The owners were having trouble making their payments because the houses' values were falling below what they owed. It was becoming a domino effect that hit the stock market and drove it down from 14,000 to just over 8,000, which had also affected Japan, China, Europe, and Russia. Oil dropped from $140 to $60 a barrel in just three months with gasoline dropping from $4.50 to just over $2 a gallon at the pumps. Hawaii hadn't felt the crunch, and our housing was still stable, but new condos that were going to be built were being put on hold.

Phil called and said two of my loans were in trouble. Christina Sage, who owed me $30,000, had gotten a divorce, and her ex wouldn't pay her any alimony. So, I'd just have to wait. Sage Hawk Development, no relation, who owed me $100,000, filed bankruptcy, leaving me with a double-wide trailer ($40,000) and the land ($80,000). Phil said I should recover the $40,000 with interest and late payments, and he would take the $60,000 balance loan himself. Normally, I would sell everything. But the value, which was worth $200,000, had dropped considerably.

George Bush gave everyone a $600 stimulus check, but it didn't stop the recession because Fannie Mae, Freddie Mac, and the banks wouldn't loan any money out to people who were being evicted from their homes every day. Even the banks were foreclosing. They should adjust the loans so people could stay in their homes and pay what they could afford. It was a buyer's market today and would be for a few years—goddamn greedy people. The big three car manufactures went to Washington in their private jets and asked Congress for $25 billion. So, Congress told them to sell their jets, quit paying their workers $75 and hour, and ask the oil companies for a loan.

On November 4, 2008, Senator Barack Obama, Democrat, and his running mate, Senator Joe Biden defeated his Republican rival, Senator John McCain, and his running mate, Alaskan Governor Sara Palin, becoming the forty-fourth president of the United States. He won by a 54 percent to 46 percent margin, mainly due to Sara Palin's inexperience. Barack Obama, who was from Hawaii, had to deal with the economy; health care; and the wars in Iraq, Afghanistan, and Pakistan. And given he'd never been a military man, it was going to be a difficult time in office.

Osama bin Laden made a statement over the internet, calling Barack a "house negro," a low form of human being, and referring him to as Malcolm X. Barack was very flamboyant like JFK was, and I was afraid someday he may be assassinated. Also Honolulu's mayor Mufi Hannemann was reelected and wanted to spend $2.5 billion on an elevated light rail system from the west side of the island to downtown Honolulu. I thought it was a waste of time and money because people were going to continue to drive their cars and clog the freeways. A cheaper way of reducing traffic would be to expand the bus system, as buses were more versatile and could get you closer to your destination.

Well, we were finally in a recession. Chrysler and General Motors had filed for bankruptcy, but Ford was very liquid. Everyone was buying everyone out. If you had a few dollars to spend, three-bedroom, two-bath houses in Hilo on the Big Island could be bought for $250,000. Unfortunately, I didn't have any cash because of those bad loans with Phil in Nevada.

Mayumi, my next-door neighbor, had her daughter Sayuri, and her two other children, Shoma and Yuina, come from Sapporo, Japan, for two week. So, I'd been playing father to a couple of kids who didn't speak English and were spoiled. I helped replace Mayumi's drapes, shower spray, and kitchen faucet, plus other problems in her condo. Sayuri, who was thirty-five years old and spoke good English, wanted to move to Hawaii. But her husband had to stay in Japan and work. She was very mature, and we'd become very friendly. I finally bought a sliding glass shower door from Glassco and had it installed for $500.

It was February 11, 2009, and the SBS LPGA at Turtle Bay started. I was a rover taking care of the front nine. Everything went well until the last day, when Beth LaGoy got on my case and I "walked." I wasn't the only one who left that Canadian cunt.

It was June and getting warmer, so I started working on the sprinkler system at DHTC that hadn't worked in years. Maybe I'd bit off more than I could chew. There were eight stations, and I'd replaced half of the sprinklers in six of the stations. But there was no water to the last two stations, and the relief valve on the fourth station didn't work. So, I drive out every other night and turned it on manually. The Parks and Recreation Department just watched and wouldn't help or didn't know how—typical locals.

I must have twisted my knee working on those damn sprinklers because I tore the meniscus on my right kneecap. I couldn't get in to see the VA, so I went to an orthopedist in Kailua named Robert Medoff. He was a neighbor of Charlie Schumucker, my golfing partner. He shot me with cortisone that made me feel like a young man, and I went out the next day and made it worse on the tennis court. Now all I could do was elevate it and ice it down, along with a little swimming and some golf. And all this because I'd volunteered to help the city; nothing was fair.

Playing golf at Klipper in Kaneohe had taken a toll on my braking system because of the steep thousand-foot pass over the Pali Highway. I wore out all the discs and shoes, costing me $1,800 for a complete brake overhaul, and had the front end rods and bushings replaced. But I should be good for a while. I also tried to have my thirty-one-year-old Goodyear Polyglas spare tire repaired, but when they filled it with air, it blew up. So, I replaced it with a forty-dollar used radial. The oil and temperature gauge on my dashboard had quit because of a brittle plastic circuit board, and Lindsey had been searching the internet with no success. So, I made sure I checked my oil and water weekly.

I finally got the Club Tsunami and Elite Electronics evicted from the Samsung Plaza, and it had never been so quiet in six years. I hoped the residents appreciated my efforts. Charlie and I had been playing golf all over the island looking for the best deals, but his health was deteriorating because of his exposure to the Agent Orange defoliant. Charlie took Mayumi and me to the fish auction at Pier 38 and bought an ahi for $1.30 a pound and an opah for $.30 a pound and then took it to his house in Kailua and showed us how to filet the fish. It was September, and the guavas, passion fruit, tangerines, and avocados were ripe for the picking on the golf courses; this was paradise.

Lisa Hwanz, my Korean friend, came back from Seoul and moved back into my building. So, I built her a kitchen counter and tiled it, making her the envy of the building. She was about sixty years old (no birth certificate) and wanted to marry me but was very demanding and cooked very spicy food that was too hot for me.

I played tennis one morning with the boys and was joined by Yuko Kido, a Japanese girl who was sixteen inches shorter and sixteen years younger than me but hit a hell of a ball. She'd been married for twenty years and had three children in their teens but was a flirt.

We finally hired a new condo manager, Atrious Alexander, who had done more improvements than any other manager. My loan in Sun Valley, Nevada, finally went into foreclosure, costing me $3,000, less $5,000 I got for a mobile home. And now I got $415 a month rent from another mobile home that was put on the property. The total loan was $105,000, but I now owned the land, which was worth about $80,000. My monthly income was $4,000 a month plus $350 a month from a loan not being paid. I reported only my pension and social security and was finally audited in 2008 and paid the taxes on the interest.

Mele Kalikimaka and Hauoli Makahiki Hou, Merry Christmas and Happy New Year. It was January 1, 2010, and the fireworks were as bad as last year. Maybe the city would ban them forever.

I pruned seventeen Manila palms this morning at DHTC without any help, and the sprinklers were running every other night on a timer that had cost me about $500. While I was replacing the sprinkler heads, I'd torn a nerve in my left hand, and my thumb and index finger went numb. So, Lisa took me to an acupuncturist for a month but without any results. I thought I needed a neural surgeon. I finally received a certificate for two hundred shares of Engle Mining that my father had bought twenty years ago and I'd misplaced. But they were still only worth about twenty-five cents a share.

Charlie and I bought a fifty-pound ahi for four dollars pound. We filleted it, and I took half and gave it to my friends in Honolulu for New Year's Eve sashimi, which would have cost them thirty dollars a pound. Sayuri and her kids arrived from Sapporo, Japan, again, but Shoma was becoming a terror and needed some discipline. I took Mayumi and her family to Charlie's in Kailua for a day at the beach and a barbecue, but they wore me out. Then Charlie's sewer line plugged, and I wound up swabbing his house, ugh!

The next day, I was showing Sayuri how to use my laptop. Shoma started pounding on the keys, and the whole thing froze up. I took it to Office Depot, and they said it had to be sent to Toshiba on the mainland for repairs, which cost me $300. I'd never have kids.

On February 26, an 8.8 earthquake hit Santiago, Chile, and a twelve-foot tsunami was headed our way and should arrive about noon tomorrow. The entire island was moving to higher ground—all except for the homeless people. I didn't know what was going to happen to them. The tsunami finally arrived but it was only about a meter high. It came and went without causing any damage but you could see the water recede before the waves came; it was quite a sight and a good learning experience.

My knee was healing slowly, so I had Dr. Ron Peroff inject it with prolotherapy, a kind of glucose, that helped a little. Keith Johnson, a tennis player friend, said he tore his meniscus twenty-five years earlier, and it took two years to completely heal by itself.

I lost another tooth due to my aircraft accident in 1982, so I had another implant put in. The crown would have to wait until October, though, as I'd maxed out my insurance coverage. On March 18, I had a lymphoma removed from my upper left back that was the size of a golf ball and had been growing for about five years (VA, no charge).

The front windshield on the Ranchero had been leaking for years, so I took it to Shon's auto body behind Lindsey's. They removed the glass and welded the corrosion that took too long, was repainted with a brush, and cost $700. Goddamn Koreans—I could have done better myself. I finally took it to the Dent Doctor and had it repainted for another $500. I never learn.

Ever since my aircraft accident I'd had ringing sounds in my head, but I'd never thought much about it until lately. Now, the troops that had returned from Iraq were complaining about the same problem due to improvised explosive devices (IEDs). So, I bought an over-the-counter pill called Ring Stop and took it for three weeks without any improvement. What a waste of money.

I turned sixty-nine in May. According to the Japanese, the sixty-ninth birthday is a yin and yang year because the numbers read the same upside down, and it might be a lucky year. Who knew? I'd known Yuko Kido for six months now, so I took her and Liki, a tennis friend, for a tour of Pearl Harbor, Submarine Base, and Hickam AFB and then treated them to dinner at the Sea Breeze Restaurant. A good time was had by all.

The following weekend, Liki invited Yuko and me over to his condo, the Liliuokalani, for tennis and dinner, where Yuko started flirting with me. A week later, I asked Yuko over for dinner but she was shocked because her Japanese custom didn't allow her to go to a man's house alone. So, we decide to go out to dinner. We went to the La Marianna on Sand Island, one of the few Hawaiian restaurants left in Honolulu. After a few beers and good conversation, I ordered the prime rib. The first bite got stuck in my throat and wouldn't go down or come up. For seven hours, I kept trying to swallow and then finally went to the emergency room at Tripler Army Hospital, where they put me on an IV with a relaxing serum and morphine until the meat finally passed into my stomach. The doctor said I had a constricted passage, probably caused by my 1982 airplane accident in Nevada.

Well, I guess Yuko is getting more comfortable with me because she finally came over to my condo for dinner and had a great time—until I tried to get close to her. Her husband worked in Tokyo and had a girlfriend and didn't see much of Yuko. In fact, Yuko hadn't had sex or an orgasm in eighteen years but thought about it often. She said she'd had a few boyfriends since she'd lived here but nothing serious. So, maybe I was a threat to her. Anyway, she couldn't get out of my condo fast enough and was very confused while I drove her home.

The following week when we played tennis together, she acted very friendly. So, I called one day and asked her out again. She told me she'd had a boyfriend for four months. What an insult. I wrote her a very stern letter about not hurting people and being up front before a relationship went too far. These Asians were not very experienced in this field.

I biked to St. Francis Hospital to have my esophagus enlarged by small balloons. Now I could eat better, and my voice was higher with more resonance. When I tried to leave the hospital, they made me take a taxi home. So, I had to drive back to pick up my bicycle—no sense of humor. The doctor told me I was not to do any exercise while I recovered. So I swam a mile that afternoon at Ala Moana—big deal.

I took Mayumi and Mitsuko to Klipper and met Charlie for a round of golf and then treated everyone to lunch. Charlie was not the same because of his deteriorating health due to the Agent Orange exposure. I saw Dr. Taylor at Tripler, who said I needed an EMG for my hand to determine if there was any nerve damage.

I took Lisa to the Pearl Harbor NEX for shopping and then dinner at my condo. Then she wanted to go out for Korean food, ugh! I tried to have sex with her later that night, but she said no. We went to Manoa

Valley the next day to meet Lisa's sister, who had been a Korean actress years ago. Then Lisa said we were going to get married. What the hell?!

I called the VA to schedule the EMG, but they were AFU. So, I saw Dr. Randolph, who got me the appointment in five minutes. Mufi Hannemann left the mayor's office to run for governor, and Kirk Caldwell took his place with a very positive attitude. I sent a letter to Dr. Hastings, head of the VA, regarding modular four and their incompetent nurse. So, maybe we'd get some results. We had a bulk item and trash problem in Honolulu, so Mufi introduced a city ordinance that, being caught stuffing bulk items into the trash would result in a $500 fine, but it never went through. So, I wrote a letter And sent it, along with pictures of the trash in our neighborhood, to Kirk Caldwell, acting mayor. Within one day, a Bill was resubmitted with a $250 fine if caught.

I was tired of the incompetent people working in our condo, so I sent a letter to the board regarding what had happened in the last seven years and asked for answers. The rental people weren't being screened and informed about the house rules, and the security system, both the cameras and the guards, needed updating. Someday, I was going to manage the building. Larry Oishi wanted to sit down and talk with me because he thought I was going to upset the management. This place had been corrupt for a long time, and someone had to challenge their authority.

Lisa, my Korean friend, was still trying to marry me. But she was too old and too bossy. I didn't know how I was going to get away from her. The city came and took the bulk item trash away in our neighborhood and said they would patrol the area because this was a hot spot for dumping.

It was July 16, 2010, Lahaina Noon, the day on which, once a year, the sun was directly overhead and there was no shadow. Lisa and her Korean friend, Nani, came over for drinks and pupus one night, and after a few gin and tonics, I said I would marry both of them, and we would all have sex together. I needed to stop drinking so much.

In August, I went to Straub Hospital through the VA for an EMG on my left hand. Then I was scheduled me a November 2 surgery.

I finally got in to see Dr. Watson at the VA for my annual physical, and all she wanted to talk about was how fucked up the Tripler Army Hospital and Department of Defense were, suggesting I should write a letter to General Eric Shinseki, head of the VA in Washington, DC. Well, Oishi had finally been relieved as condo management, and we were now under Hawaiian First.

On October 12, 2010, thirty miners from Copiapó, Chile, were stuck in a caved-in mine two thousand feet below the surface. They managed to find an area the size of my condo and survived for sixty-nine days, until, with the help of the United States, they were rescued one by one by way of a bullet-shaped pod sent down a drilled hole.

Delta Dental finally covered the rest of my implant and crown, which looked as good as the rest of my teeth. We had a midterm election on November 2, 2010, and all the Republicans in Hawaii except one were replaced by Democrats. But the Republicans at least took over the house in Washington, DC, and Speaker of the House Nancy Pelosi was replaced by Senator John Boehner, thank God.

I went to Tripler and had carpal tunnel surgery done on my left hand to try and bring back the feeling in my thumb. But it put me out of commission for a week. It seemed every time I got sick, my car also got sick. I had the head and oil pan gaskets replaced for $700. The electrical unit in my fridge burned, so I ordered a GE from the mainland for $900. HECO's substation next to our condo exploded because of the rain and lack of installation.

I helped Jasmine Ige tile number 1809 and charged her $500. Resurfacing of DHTC courts started January 4 and ended July 4, costing about $90,000. Of that, $30,000 came from donations, $30,000 from the city, and $30,000 was from the USTA.

McCain paid off her loan, and then I refinanced Hosking at $300 per month at 5 percent and Martinez at $400 per month at 5 percent. But Christina Sage hadn't paid me anything in years. Maybe I'd foreclose. I finally hung my LCD TV on the wall and bought a cabinet for $250 at City Mill that sold for $1,000 in furniture stores.

On July Fourth, Ala Moana Beach was so crowded I decided to bike up Manoa Valley to Paradise Park and hike an hour to Manoa

Falls, meeting a lot of friendly people on the way. My air conditioner in the Ranchero started leaking and would cost $3,000 to overhaul. So, I bought a stop leak kit and fixed it myself for $70. My condo had become infested with fruit flies from our trash chute. I had Sandwich Isle Pest Control spray my condo and install a bug light for $600 because of our incompetent resident manager and spent the night at the Sub Base BOQ for $55.

I wrote a letter to the army surgeon general in Virginia regarding the lack of communications between Triple Army Hospital and the VA, pointing out that, even though they were in the same building, their computers weren't linked up, making it hard to schedule doctors. I went to Straub and got a physical from Dr. Nekemoto, who said he'd been seeing a lot of veterans who were also unhappy with the VA. But because I'd never opted for Medicare Part B, it would take a year to become eligible for TRICARE for Life. So, I decided to give the VA another try if they got rid of a very inept nurse, which they did.

When I lived in Reno, the VA was run like a fine-tuned watch. If you needed an operation, the VA would fly you down to San Jose to a specialist from Stanford University.

The new management of Hawaii First and the board of directors at Holiday Village applied for a $1 million loan to update our elevators and fire alarm system because there was no reserve set aside after forty-seven years. Marcia Kimura, an owner, and I brought in Richard Port, an expert on condominium affairs to help contact the owners who didn't live in the building and solicit their proxies. We held a special meeting on November 23, 2011, to replace the board of directors but could only come up with 38 percent of the votes. It was better than anyone had expected. So maybe we could do better next March at the annual meeting. This board had held these proxies for too long; it was time for a change.

On December 4, 2011, I received a call from USAA. Someone had tried to buy $700 worth of merchandise on line at a boutique in Los Angeles using my visa number, but when they gave an LA address, USAA had stopped the purchase. People were breaking into computers all over the nation extracting credit card numbers; nothing was safe anymore. It was that time of year, so I pruned the Manila palms and plumeria trees at DHTC and planted more grass.

New Year's 2012 was quiet and smokeless due to the ban on fireworks, thank god. I got sick from a mango I' picked up on the West Lock Golf Course that had black spots. I suffered from vomiting and diarrhea for three days; you don't get something for nothing. Sandwich Isle came to spray the condo and change the bug light strip and found more than two hundred bugs.

I drafted a letter to two hundred condo owners with Richard Port's help and received over forty proxies for the annual meeting. On January 28, 2012, I got sideswiped on my bicycle by a flatbed truck at Kalakaua and Kapahulu. The collision fractured my clavicle and put a gash in my head. It was a hit-and-run, and nobody saw the license plate, as the driver was speeding and pulling a trailer. I was taken to Queen's Hospital for X-rays and staples in my skull and then released three hours later. And can you believe the total bill was $6,000?

The VA wouldn't cover it because I had Tri Care, and Tri Care wouldn't cover it because I didn't have Medicare Part B. So, I contacted USAA. They said I was covered under a personal injury protection plan and paid everything with no deductible; maybe being with them for forty-seven years helped.

Well, for the next week, I licked my wounds and tried to exercise my left shoulder so it wouldn't freeze up like Tilly's had in Reno, leaving him with restricted movement for the rest of his life.

In January 2011, I bought sixteen-ounce bags of Planters pistachios at Pearl Harbor Commissary for $2.69 per pound. Six months later, they were $3.49 per pound. Then in January 2012, I ordered another case, but when they arrived there were only nine bags in the box, and the bags were reduced to 12.75 ounces and sold for almost $6 per pound. Well, that was enough for me to get some answers. I contacted the commissary manager, and he said that was the price he received, and they only put a surcharge on their products at no profit. I wrote a letter to Kraft Foods, who distributed the nuts for Planters, and they told me they hadn't raised their prices either. So who was in the middle making a profit that had almost tripled in one year?

I wrote a letter to the Better Business Bureau, who referred me to the BBB in Illinois, where Kraft Foods' headquarters were. After a month, nobody would give an explanation and closed the case. So, I went to the Department of Commerce and Consumer Affairs and was referred to the executive director of a sales marketing and policy group in Virginia. I received a letter from the military team at Kraft Foods, but all they said was that, when I'd first bought their nuts in 2011, the price was under a promotional package. Nobody wanted to admit they were price gouging.

I ran for the 2012 board of directors in March, but the board added Mike Adams's name so I couldn't get all the votes. I started attending the monthly meetings, but it was the same old shit, so I was washing my hands of this condo management. Hawaii First had been sent $4,000 for elevator renovation and the fire alarm system, but six months had passed, and they hadn't worked on the elevator yet. What a scam. The board kept changing its meeting times so nobody would show up. They were just a bunch of assholes.

My shoulder was getting stronger by swimming, including the butterfly and lifting weights. Tripler did an MRI and found my rotator cup was undamaged, so I'd just have a bone sticking up when I didn't walk straight.

I helped Eddie Thompson, a tennis friend plant a lawn in his front yard, but he wouldn't water it so it looked like shit. No more Mister Nice Guy.

My right knee was sore again after three years with prolotherapy shots. So I had it shot again by Ron Peroff, an ENT. This time it didn't work, so I quit playing tennis and changed my physical activities. Now, I swam and played golf more and would let someone else take care of the tennis courts. But that would never happen; nobody likes to volunteer.

We had a downpour one day in June, and brown, smelly liquid came down from a unit above me and covered every lanai down to the first floor. I mentioned it to the manager, but he just sat in his office and asked me what I wanted him to do. I went up and knocked on number 1001, and Donna Lee, a friend of mine, answered the door. She said she'd been having pigeon problems, and when I looked under the air conditioner, it was the most disgusting sight I'd seen—two baby pigeons sitting on a pile of waste a foot high. Since the condo management wasn't going to do anything Midge, Donna, and I put on masks and rubber gloves, and on Independence Day, we worked for four hours removing those pigeons and cleaning her lanai. The board immediately started inspecting the lanais again for AC drip trays that would have prevented the birds from nesting in the first place. Now they were nervous because I told them I would take legal action against the board, the manager, and Hawaii First for dereliction of duty—let them sweat.

I went to Tripler, and the orthopedist said the meniscus had torn loose, and I might need arthroscopic surgery. I had another close call on my bike with these crazy drivers, so I gave the bike to a Philippine boy in my building, and now I walk everywhere.

Eight months later, the pain in my knee started to subside, so I went back to Tripler. The doctor said the meniscus had repaired itself, so no surgery, and I was back on the tennis courts. But now I played at Ala Moana because Diamond Head was too far away.

The city finally painted a bike lane through Waikiki, but there still wasn't enough room with the cars; this island was just too small. Since I cleaned Donna's lanai, bird mites had invaded my apartment and were biting and hatching in my skin. In fact, they had nested around my left eye. I had my place fumigated, but the bugs were still there. I went to my dermatologist who gave me some pills and skin cream, but it wasn't working; this had been going on for over a year.

Six months ago, I'd finally had sex with Lisa, but there was an odor coming from my penis. I had to see a urologist, who said I picked up a fungus. It cost me $500 for treatment; that was the end of that relationship.

I gave Keoki Ching at Edward Jones $25,000 for a diversified investment, hoping he'd make me some money. I had another $25,000 with Nationwide that was drawing 3 percent, but I couldn't touch it until March 2014 without a penalty.

On November 29, 2012, I got my first "hole in one" at the West Loch Golf Course on the par 3 seventh and then took Ray and Norman to lunch. Mayor Kirk Caldwell, newly in office, was cleaning up our city's bulk trash, repaving roads, and helping the homeless. I hoped he wouldn't run out of energy.

Lindsey, my mechanic, had cancer and closed down his shop. So, I found Malcomb at Punahou Auto near my condo. He fixed my loose steering, adjusted my gear linkage, overhauled the carburetor, replaced the rotor and spark plug wires, and found an instrument panel on the internet. He liked working on old cars. He said the Japanese had a universal air conditioner that would replace my original. I tried to reregister my car as a classic to save $200 a year. But that would require me to call the DMV for a permit every time I drove. It wasn't worth the hassle.

I started writing the Regulated Industries Complaint Office (RICO) at the beginning of the year regarding questions I'd asked the condo board and Hawaii First without receiving any answers. RICO was a state-run facility, so my next step was to contact the governor's office. I finally received a letter from RICO—they were still working on my case because of a possible criminal offense regarding someone from our board tampering with the voting ballots. I'd get those bastards eventually, but RICO couldn't represent me, so I may have to hire a lawyer.

Nobody wanted to touch my instrument panel, so I pulled it out myself. The plastic was so brittle it crumbled in my hands. Malcomb finally found one in Texas on eBay with an asking price of $35. But a day later someone bid $100, and I told Malcomb to keep bidding. After two days, I finally won the bid, but that instrument panel cost me $450. After it arrived, I disassembled it, sealed the plastic with fusion paint, cannibalized some of the instruments from my panel, put it back together, and installed it in my car without any help, not bad for an old guy. Malcomb said the Ranchero was now worth about $20,000.

I met Alan Leong at Ala Wai Golf Course and told him about my Ranchero and how I'd installed another instrument panel, but the speedometer didn't work. He said to bring it over to his house in Kaimuki. When I arrived, there was a '31 Ford Roadster and a '42 Ford Coupe in his front yard with tools everywhere. He crawled under my car and loosened the cable, and I secured it to the speedometer in the dash.

Fifteen minutes later, everything was working for the first time in five years, and I had to force him to take some money. He also tried to repair some corrosion on the bottom of the passenger door, but I eventually took it to Chuck's Auto, which cost me $500. The only problem left was the heater / air-conditioning control.

Representative John Mizuno contacted me regarding sending a homeless man who said he'd been promised a job here in Hawaii back to Albuquerque, New Mexico. I met with everyone at the state building and matched John's $100 toward a $500 ticket to send the guy back to New Mexico. Maybe other citizens would do the same in the future.

We had our building painted for the first time in forty-five years, but I had to cut down my lilikoi plant after five years. I guess it would grow back.

On November 1, 2013, I bought 153 shares of Potash from Edward Jones for $33 per share, leaving my balance at $32,000.

I'd repaired all five tennis nets at Ala Moana, but someone kept stealing the center straps. If things weren't secured on this island, they disappeared in a minute. Representative Tom Brower was fed up with the homeless, so he took a sledgehammer to the streets to rid the homeless of their shopping carts. I wrote him a letter and told him I'd been chasing the homeless out of our neighborhood for years and thanked him for his efforts.

The AC / heater control unit broke. As I didn't have access to the internet, I went to the main library and was able to use the computers for free. I located a control unit through Google at Desert Valley Wrecking in Phoenix, Arizona, and had it delivered to me for $70. Malcomb at Punahou Auto installed it for $200 and said he ordered a new compressor and evaporator that were made in Japan.

Every year, I would go down to the federal building and have the IRS do my taxes. But in 2014, because of budget cuts, there were no more freebies. I found Jackson Hewitt at Walmart, who charged me $250 but saved me $500 on my return.

The air conditioner in my condo was getting louder and wouldn't drain properly, but because I had it reinstalled at the top of the window, I no longer could work on it myself. Cool Zone picked it up and had to replace the fan motor, which I'm sure was due to poor draining. They reinstalled it after I asked them to tilt the AC more. Now, it was quiet and it drained the way it should, but it cost me $260. The motor in my Kenmore vacuum cleaner had been getting louder every year, so I tried to get it fixed. But it was beyond repair. Not bad for finding it ten years ago in our building. I bought a good used Kenmore for $120.

Sayuri and her kids, Shoma, Yuina, and now Yo, had returned from Sapporo for a couple of weeks. But I didn't have to be a tour guide this time.

In March 2014, I transferred another $26,525 from Nationwide Annuity to Edward Jones, which was only getting me a 3 percent return. Keoki from Edward Jones had been getting me 15 percent or better with stocks and bonds, making my investment worth $64,000.

Pro Park, Inc. the garage where I parked my car, raised the monthly rent to $130 from $95. Everything on this island was getting expensive, but it was paradise. I had the radiator and battery on the car replaced for $500. For years, the car had been smoking when I started it and burned a quart of oil every thousand miles, so I decided to have the valve stem seals replaced. But it was causing the engine to backfire because the valves had to reseat themselves or have the heads removed and overhauled. I'd drive it for a while. I also had a new compressor, evaporator, and hoses installed on the AC—first time it had worked in years.

An old replica of a Hawaiian sailing boat, *Hokulea*, with a crew of fifteen, left Oahu May 23, 2014, attempting to sail around the world navigating only by the stars and ocean currents; it should take about a year.

Phil Hosking called from Reno and said I now had a first deed of trust on the Sage property but had to start paying the taxes on the Martinez property because he'd vacated and stopped making the loan payments. New condos were going up all over Honolulu. Some penthouses were selling for as much as $15 million, with most of the buyers coming from China and paying cash. We were headed for becoming the most expensive real estate market in the nation. I was fortunate I'd bought my condo ten years ago because, since then, the price had doubled.

On September 1, 2014, there was an Ebola outbreak in Western Africa that could spread throughout the world without a vaccine; until January 2015, just keep travelers out of our country.

Tesla, the automaker, had leased land east of Reno to build a battery plant that would hire 6,500 employees. Maybe my property would finally increase again. Malcomb was still trying to find out why my car backfired, so I bought a new carburetor. But Midas did a lousy job installing it, and now the transmission wouldn't shift. I took it to All Trans, where I met Mike Ferrar, the owner. Mike told me his father knew Malcomb's father and said to watch out for the boys at Punahou Auto. Mike fixed the transmission linkage to the carburetor; changed the sparkplug wires, the sparkplugs; and a vacuum hose from the transmission to the carburetor; fixed the choke; and retimed the engine—all in one day—and it ran better than it had in over ten years. Unfortunately, Malcomb needed to finish my AC. And after six months it was finally working, but the bill was $3,600. Why did I let everyone take advantage of me?

The 2015 New Year's celebration was the quietest since I'd moved here because the city had banned the use of fireworks. Well, we had a new governor, David Ige, who had a financial background. Maybe he'd lower the government budget. Our former governor, Neil Abercrombie, had gone on a spending spree during his time in office.

I had a short in the car stereo. I took it to Security Sound Systems, who jiggled some wires and found the problem at no charge. Alan and I installed a new air cleaner and breather hose and adjusted the belt on the power steering unit.

Tom Tanaka invited me to his birthday party at Moanawili near Kailua. The party was held at a house on five acres in the jungle with two hundred guests. I found a lilikoi plant at Tripler Army Hospital and picked enough for my beer and everyone at the condo. I had my taxes done by Jackson Hewitt and saved another $250. The AC in the car quit again. I took it to Malcomb, and he fixed it at no charge. But he knew he'd never see me again.

Mayor Kirk Caldwell held a meeting at the McCoy Pavilion in Ala Moana Beach Park regarding upgrading the park because I'd sent a letter and pictures to the Hawaii Tourism Authority and to the builders of a multimillion-dollar condo across the street. Instead of getting rid of the homeless, hoodlums, and high school dropouts who were vandalizing the park, the mayor wanted to spend $1 million for a study to build new structures. What an asshole. Eventually, the owners of those condos, who were paying up to $10 million for a six thousand-square-foot apartment, would clean up the park at their own expense so they'd have a better view.

Tripler Army Medical Center invited me to lunch at the Hickam Officers' Club, where I was awarded top donor of 2014 again. I tore the meniscus on my right knee again and had an injection of Synvisc, but the knee locked up and I couldn't walk for a couple of days. The VA scheduled me for an MRI, but who knew when that would happen? So, I swam, played golf riding a cart, and exercised as much as possible. A tennis player told me to try glucosamine, an over-the-counter pill, that worked wonder; now the pain was finally gone.

I was leaving my parking garage on the fourth floor when the brakes failed, so I limped to Midas, and they found the strap on the muffler had broken and rubbed through the power steering hose—probably caused by years of our rough roads. the damage was $350. The highways on this island were in terrible shape and had taken a toll on my car.

The State Department audited me again for not paying taxes for 2008. That cost me $930. I think they screwed me.

Mike Adams, my next-door neighbor, helped me repair the fiberglass cover on my car and a new seal that had been broken for ten years. So, I took Mike and his wife Vivian to the La Mariana for lunch.

The meniscus was still torn, so I quit playing tennis for a few months. The French Solar Impulse 2 flew in from Japan, attempting an around the world flight. The battery system heated, so they were going to stay at Barbers Point for the winter during repairs.

The knee was finally healing. I met Max Pavon, who taught tennis at Punahou for twenty years. Now I was getting free lessons at Ala Moana and the shitheads were jealous because I was getting better.

In fact, one day, Max and I beat Brian and Dean 6 to 0. After that, they wouldn't play with us anymore. Who cares? Max has improved my backhand. I was playing the best tennis I'd ever played, and I was seventy-five years old.

A new condo, the Waihonua, went up across the street from the tennis courts, but the reflectivity from the windows was blinding. I contacted HCDA, the mayor, the *Star-Advertiser*, and the neighborhood board. But the city fucked up for not checking the windows before they were installed.

The construction of buildings in Honolulu had gone wild, with a new condo going up every year. My window AC started leaking, so I tried to drill a drain hole but hit the compressor and bled out all the Freon. Cool Zone found me a used one for $250 and told me not to take on projects myself. I took the instrument panel out of the Ranchero and fixed all the gauges and then replaced the back lighting with higher wattage bulbs. For the first time in thirty-seven years, I could finally see the instruments at night. I had to have the front end aligned and found out that some front end parts needed replacing in the future, Image that had been caused by the roads in Hawaii. So I wrote a letter to the Department of Transportation, and they said it wasn't their fault—assholes.

It was 2016, and all the Republicans and Democrats were throwing their hats in for the presidency, including Donald Trump. I wrote a letter to Barack Obama regarding his poor performance over the past eight years and asked him to resign, or he might be impeached for dereliction of duty. The Dow Jones had dropped to 16,000 because of that asshole. ISIS terrorists were killing everyone in the world, including Americans, and Barack didn't know how to stop it and wouldn't ask his military advisors.

I started playing tennis at Makiki Park, but the nets were in terrible condition. So, I fixed all four of them, and the locals couldn't figure where the repairs had come from. Maybe they thought the Parks and Recreation Department did it. If you wanted anything done on this island, you had to do it yourself. I met a lot of new friends there, including local sisters Tiki and Jackie, who wanted to hit every Saturday and wore me out because it was two against one. But I didn't mind because it was good exercise.

Mike Ferrar at All Trans Transmission, who had a restored '57 Chevy, a '68 Camaro, and a '59 Thunderbird, replaced my distributor with a built-in electronic ignition, giving it more power. I had the engine cleaned and installed chrome valve covers and a chrome air cleaner, saving $250 by doing it myself. The car had been appraised at $14,000, but I'd had offers for more from the locals.

Max and I started playing singles and he was running my ass off. I wasn't sure how much I could take, but I was going to beat him some day. Unfortunately, my lower back finally gave out from the compressed discs caused by the aircraft accident in 1982, and my hole left side hurt like hell, so I'd been laid up for a week.

Finally able to walk, I went to the VA. The doctors there gave me Voltaren cream to relax the muscles, tendons, and cartilages. I wore a knee brace so I could get around. I guess I'd be off the courts for a while. Swimming in the ocean seemed to be the best therapy for now, but it took a month to get back on the golf course. Max called and said the doctors had found cancer in the lymph nodes in his neck, and he had to take radiation and chemotherapy treatments for a couple of months. So, he may never again be the tennis pro he once had been.

Donald Trump had been elected the forty-fifth president of the United States, beating out more than a dozen other Republicans who were running against him. Now the Republicans in the Senate and House who had been against him were trying to make amends—what a bunch of hypocritical assholes. Donald had no political or military experience but the white, middle-class, working-class voters liked him for his honesty, which was hard to find in the White House anymore.

Hillary Clinton was trying to buy her way into the election with her corrupt money. But the public knew she was a manipulating liar and possibly responsible for killing Ambassador Stevens and three other Americans in the massacre at the Benghazi raid in Libya when she was Secretary of State.

Donald Trump didn't need the money. He just wanted to make America great again by stopping the wars, lowering our taxes, changing

Obamacare, kicking out all the illegal immigrants, and draining the swamp in Washington. I wished him luck.

The democrats weren't too happy. Nor were the people who'd voted for Hillary and were demonstrating from coast to coast like a bunch of immature idiots. Barack Obama left the country and wouldn't talk with Donald to help him transition to the presidency on January 24, 2017. What a jerk.

After the November 8 election, we lost our last Republican senator in Hawaii, making us a pure Democratic state. So, I sent a letter to Donald regarding who to hire and who to fire. Maybe it would help. Two weeks later, I received a response from Donald and Melania thanking me for encouraging him not to give up by citing my aircraft accident in 1982.

It was 2017, and I finally foreclosed on the property in Silver Springs, Nevada, that had cost me $2,200 to file and $4,400 to have an old mobile home removed and the property cleaned up. A realtor in the area said the property was worth $35,000. But when Elon Musk, owner of Tesla Motors, finished his ten million-square-foot factory there next year, the property would be worth $50,000. I figured I'd wait.

I also received an offer on my property in Sun Valley, Nevada, from my renter for $60,000. But I thought it was worth $80,000, so I'd wait on that also. My original loan on that property had been for $100,000; I had received $30,000 in note payments and rent. So what was the hurry? If Donald Trump did what he'd promised to our country, property values should finally start increasing again.

On the negative side, Christina Sage, who I had a second deed of trust loan on was foreclosed by the loaner with the first deed and left me with a $27,000 loss. That's life.

Four months had passed, and Max and I were healing up and back on the courts again. But he was getting cranky because of his cancer. At West Loch Golf Course, I met Bob Nordstrom, a retired air force colonel who flew in Korea; we had a lot in common and became good friends. In fact, he invited me for dinner with his German wife of fifty-six years at his house in Makakilo. I brought him some of my homemade beer.

Dr. Fancher took a biopsy from the right side of my face and found a trace of cancer; the plan was to follow up next month. On March 1, 2017, my right ear started hurting twenty-four hours a day, so I went to see Dr. McManaman at the VA. She said both the inner and outer drums were blocked. She gave me some eardrops. But after a week, the pain continued. I went to see Ron Peroff, an ENT and tennis friend of mine, and he spent fifteen minutes sucking all the trash out of my ear. That reduced the pain. Ron said the VA should have done this first before adding any eardrops.

The VA finally sent me next door to the Tripler ENT Department. A CT scan found three polyps growing inside the ear that were probably caused by swimming in the ocean over the years. But the department's chief doctor was on indefinite sick leave, so I was referred to Dr. Kevin Hadley. an ENT at the Pali Momi Health Center. He couldn't get me in until July. I saved money going to the VA, but sometimes it took a while to get anything done.

On April 4, 2017, the Syrian leader Basar Assad dropped Sarin gas, killing hundreds of women and children. So Donald launched fifty-nine Tomahawk missiles at a southern airport in Syria. Then, on April 12, 2017, Secretary of Defense General James "Mad Dog" Mattis dropped a 21,000-pound MOAB bomb on the caves and tunnels in northern Afghanistan that killed ninety ISIS fighters. Then Donald went to Saudi Arabia and made a $150 billion arms deal with the king. He next went to the NATO summit and told everybody to pay their fair share, especially Merkle of Germany, who he didn't like. then he was on to Rome to see the Pope to make amends. What the hell had Obama done for the past eight years?

I dropped my car off at All Trans and had Mike install an aluminum intake manifold and a four-barrel carburetor and replace the collar and coupler on the steering shaft. Now the car went like hell, was lighter, and the steering and shifting were tighter than when it was new thirty-nine years ago. And it cost me. But the value of the car had just increased.

I went back to Tripler ENT. The polyps had disappeared with the use of the steroid eardrops. What a relief.

President Trump passed a temporary immigration ban, but the attorney general in Hawaii was protesting because he was Asian and was afraid all his relatives would be deported. This island was infested with illegal immigrants. Bob Nordstrom gave me a flyer produced by the *Star-Advertiser* called YAH (Young At Heart), and there was an article about a retired World War II pilot living in Waikiki still driving his car and playing golf. He was ninety-nine years old. I had a long way to go.

President Kim Jong-un of North Korea was launching rockets into the Sea of Japan and working on a nuclear weapon, hoping someday he'd be able to reach Hawaii and the US mainland. So we'd been updating our missile defense systems in Alaska, Southern California, and Kauai and stationing three aircraft carriers off the coast of Korea.

On October 15, 2017, there was a shooter on the thirty-second floor of the Mandalay Bay in Las Vegas who opened fire on a concert crowd two hundred yards away, killing fifty-eight and injuring hundreds before the LVPD shot and killed him. No motive was found. On Halloween, a US citizen from Uzbekistan drove a rented truck onto a bike path in Manhattan, killing eight people and injuring dozens before he was shot and captured, with ISIS claiming responsibility. There was so much information being hacked on the internet it was impossible to track the bad guys. President Trump took off for Japan, South Korea, China, Vietnam, and the Philippines for his first trip to Asia since being elected. He also stopped in Hawaii for a Military Pacific conference but had nothing to say to our pathetic Democrats. I predict that, someday, our Republicans will overcome the Democrats and make this state a better place to live.

On July 14, 2017, a fire in the Marco Polo Condominium in Waikiki killed three people and took five hours to put out. Now, the city was requiring sprinklers in all condos, which included the Holiday Village, even though we had a fire hose and extinguisher on every floor. The cost could run up to $10,000 per unit, so the city council was working on a compromise.

I had the VA inject Synvisc in right knee, but my body rejected it. My knee swelled up like a softball, so I had it drained. The doctors injected a lesser dose of Euflexxa, which worked better. One day, while going back for a lob at Ala Moana Tennis Courts, I tripped and fell on my tailbone, which grounded me for two months. The VA sent me to a back specialist at Kaukini Hospital, who looked at my X-ray and said my spine was in the shape of an S with crushed discs from all my accidents. No surgery was needed, but I was to just slow down; I wasn't thirty-five anymore.

After ten years, my reclining chair finally broke, so I fixed it and then gave it to the Salvation Army. I found a new one at Navy Exchange and saved $500.

President Trump still had a low approval rating in 2017, even though the stock market was at an all-time high (26,000), the unemployment was at the lowest, and the economy was thriving. Let's hope 2018 would be better.

One day, the bacteria level at Ala Moana Beach spiked a hundred times the normal level, but the health department put up a sign a day after my swim. I had stomach and gastronomic pains for forty-eight hours, and the doctors couldn't find the source. Our sewer system hadn't kept up with all the massive building of condos. Someday, we may have polluted oceans like South America does.

An employee at the US Pacific Command emergency office pushed the wrong button and sent out a message that a missile was inbound from North Korea. But it took thirty minutes to notify everyone that it was a false alarm. All the political leaders on this island had no idea what was going on. So, I sent President Trump a letter regarding "draining the swamp in Hawaii."

On February 26, 2018, the city finally resurfaced the tennis courts and added new nets as part of the beautification of Ala Moana Reginal Park. Phil Hosking called and said he had someone who wanted to put a mobile home on my property in Silver Springs, Nevada. The area was growing due to all the factories moving in, including Amazon, Yahoo, and Tesla. A storm came through in April, and it rained twenty-six inches in twenty-four hours on Kauai, a record.

President Trump got President Moon Jae-in of South Korea to meet with President Kim Jong-un and sign a peace agreement for the first time in sixty-five years. Now, President Trump had set up a meeting with Kim Jong-un sometime in May of this year to discuss denuclearization. Trump had done more in eighteen months than Obama had in eight years.

I found a mechanic at Midas who had a '67 Chevy Camaro and said he would rewire my instrument panel—what a relief. Bob Nordstrom and I were finally playing golf again after six months of his sore back (for which he never found the cause). Goddess Madam Pele was getting angry again on the Big Island, with eruptions of Mt. Kilauea causing evacuations of 1,800 people. Hawaii is one of two hot spots in the world, the other being Yellowstone National Park, which was also showing some activity.

President Trump met with President Kim Jong-un June 12, 2018, on an island off Singapore. They shook hands and signed an agreement; if Kim denuclearized his country the United States would lift the sanctions against North Korea and stop the military exercises with South Korea; we shall see. President Trump's next meeting was with Vladimir Putin in August.

After a year and a half of temperature fluctuations in my water system, I wrote a letter to Ann Kobayashi of the Honolulu City Council, and our condo association had been working day and night trying to fix the problem. It's not what you know but who you know.

The Supreme Court finally passed Trump's immigration ban, and all the illegal immigrants in Hawaii were nervous about getting deported. It was about time. They'd been sneaking into our islands for decades.

I made a hole in one on the par 3 fifth, 106 yards, with an eight iron at West Loch Golf Course and took Bob to lunch at Chilis in Kapolei. North Korea sent fifty-five boxes of American remains to Pearl Harbor / Hickam for identification of the '51-'53 war. Phil Hosking, my financial adviser, passed away on October 12, 2018, so his estate paid off his loan to me for $10,000.

On October 25, 2018, I had a severe pain in my urinary tract for a week, but my primary doctor at the VA couldn't find the problem. So, a week later, I finally went to the ER at Tripler. The doctors there found a kidney stone that started near my kidney and eventually lodged at the bottom of my urinary tract. I couldn't get into surgery for three days, so I took pain pills while playing tennis and golf. The stone was removed by laser, and a stent was installed in my ureteral tract for a week for healing—what a painful experience. While I was laid up, my car was also sick and needed a carburetor overhaul; it seemed the both of us got sick together.

The Delta Dental program I had was switching to a new program, but I needed a computer and Gmail address to enroll. So a tennis friend, Tom Tanaka, helped me but said I needed to buy an iPhone. Soon, everyone was tracking everything I did on that phone; there was no privacy anymore. On December 2, 2018, President George H. W. Bush passed away at the age of ninety-four.

In all, 2018 had been a very busy year for hurricanes. When Lane had been heading straight for Oahu, the whole island shut down for three days, preparing for the worst. But at the last hour, the hurricane veered to the south and dissipated. Someday, we'd get hit.

It was 2019, and Donald finally started building the wall on the southern border. But when Central America heard about it, immigrants came in caravans of a thousand or more, and Mexico couldn't stop them. Congress wouldn't help because the Democrats hated Donald Trump, but the situation was so rampant that an American who was smuggling two Chinese was shot to death by the border patrol. And intelligence heard that an ISIS individual booked a flight from Afghanistan to Guatemala. His plan was to ride in a caravan to the US border and be smuggled into the United States. He would then head toward New York to work at a high-value business building, eventually creating massive destruction in the city. Wake up, Nancy Pelosi, and your incapable Democratic House.

In June, the largest and most powerful telescope in the world was scheduled to be put atop Mauna Kea on the Big Island, but hundreds of local Hawaiians set up camp and blocked the road so construction couldn't begin. Our governor and the mayor of Hawaii Island wouldn't help because some of the protesters were their relatives. So far, it had cost taxpayers $11 million, mostly for law enforcement.

A huge storm created a landslide on the Pali Highway, which would be shut down for six months, affecting businesses in Kailua. Two accidents involving the Boeing 737 MAX 8 killed 350 people in

Indonesia and Ethiopia. So, I wrote a letter to Dennis Muilenburg, CEO of Boeing, explaining that the cause of those accidents was the lack of experience and training on high-tech aircraft in third world countries. And it would only get worse.

Ryan Phillips called from Nevada and had some investors who wanted to buy my property in Silver Springs. I told him I would take $36,000 and finance the deal at 10 percent interest for at least a year, giving me another $5,000. Linda Burgess, who owned a double-wide trailer on my property in Sun Valley, had been paying me $415 a month for five years. But she was diagnosed with breast cancer and wanted to sell the trailer and move to Yarington with her children. I gave her $15,000 and rented the trailer to her grandson for $1,200 a month, giving me a value of $180,000 for the property and trailer if I ever decided to sell.

Fred at Midas installed a new Eldebrock carburetor, but on the way home from the golf course, the throttle stuck at sixty-five miles per hour. So, I put it in neutral, pulled off to the side of the highway, and temporarily fixed the linkage. Then I drove to All Trans and had Mike repair it—no more Midas.

The Democrats in the House were trying to impeach Trump for everything he did. They acted act like a bunch of children.

I replaced all the halogen lights in my track lighting in the condo with LED because the transformer was getting hot. I drew up another will in 2019, with Dolores Johnson as my heiress. I now had two wills, the first one made in 1999, with Scott Sheridan as my heir. So, maybe the two could split my assets. My tennis friend and mentor Keith Johnson, a retired navy captain, just turned ninety-six years old, and his daughter-in-law, a retired three-star general, pulled rank and moved him to a nursing home in Seattle after forty years in Hawaii. That would never happen to me, thank God.

In November, I started losing strength in my left shoulder and bicep. Then a week later, I irritated my sciatica on the tennis court, which was probably a godsend because I'd been overdoing it physically lately.

I finally took my car to Lex Brodie's for a complete brake work, and it ran great for half the cost of Midas, who'd overcharged me for shoddy work for years. I complained to the head office in Florida, but because they were a franchised store, I never received any restitution, except for a free oil change. Good and fair-priced mechanics on the island were hard to find. I found LED lights at O'Reilly's Auto Parts that were brighter and cooler, and I could finally see my instrument panel in the Ranchero at night after forty years.

Financially, 2019 was a pretty good year. I sold one property in Nevada, and I was receiving three times the rent on the other. Donald gave the military a raise. And the value of my condo and car kept increasing. Now it was 2020, and the hateful Democrats in congress were still trying to impeach the president. But Donald kept moving forward building the wall, lowering unemployment, creating a new Space Force, increasing his popularity, and trying to keep peace in the world.

For decades, a top warmongering general in Iran had been attacking and killing Americans. So, last week, Donald Trump sent a Hellfire missile from a drone that exterminated him in Iraq. The Iranians retaliated by launching rockets toward our bases in Iraq, but they accidentally shot down a Ukraine airliner with 176 passengers on board, mostly Iranians, killing their own protesters on the ground in the process. The death toll was over 2,000 people. Instead of starting a war, our secretary of the treasury put more sanctions on Iran to eventually bring the Iranians to the peace table.

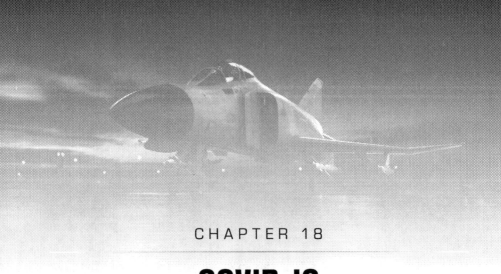

CHAPTER 18

COVID-19

In November 2019, a corona virus developed in Wuhan, China, from the selling of live exotic animals in open wet markets. The animals were kept in cages stacked on top of one another, allowing their waste to drip down, creating the virus. They were selling bats, snakes, rats, lizards, and the like, something that had been going on for decades. But China wouldn't declare the virus existed until January 6, 2020, at which point it was killing ten people a day from blood clotting and lung and pneumonia problems.

By the time we found out about it, the virus was spreading all over the world. So, Donald Trump immediately cancelled all flights coming to the United States from China on January 8. That probably saved thousands of American lives. But the House Democrats criticized him; what a bunch of assholes.

I had a new Interstate battery installed in the Ranchero after six years. I also had a single valve installed in my condo shower and found the old tee pipe was corroded. That cost $900, but now the water temperature didn't oscillate for the first time in four years. I guess I'm too stubborn. Chuck's Auto Body repaired rust on the lower car door for $2,300. So, I sent the claim to USAA, but they wouldn't cover rust damage—oh well.

The House Democrats finally sent the impeachment of Donald Trump to the Senate, but it was turned down. What a waste of time and our tax money. It was January 17, 2020, and the virus that had been named COVID-19 was killing twenty people a day from human-to-human contact; it was being passed just by people breathing on one another. So, people were starting to wear face masks.

On February 8, deaths were up to 900 worldwide. On February 13, the death toll hit 1,100. And the virus was declared an epidemic. My sciatica still hurt because of golf, so I tried to slow down my swing, which helped a little. Even swimming seemed to help as long as I didn't do the butterfly stroke.

On February 29, the United States had its first COVID-19 death, with the world at a death toll of 3,000. On March 6, Hawaii had its first case. People were starting to get nervous. So, I wrote a letter to Governor Ige because he was too slow, as usual, to react to the problem and suggested he stop tourists from coming to our island. On March 12, the world death toll was 5,000, and Hawaiians were buying toilet paper by the shopping cart load. Then someone put out a bad rumor that Matson Shipping Lines were closed. When I got to the Hickam Commissary, people were lined up into the parking lot. Needless to say, the store was cleaned out that day. Then we found out the rumor was false.

On March 1, I wrote a letter to President Xi Jinping, telling him I met President Jiang Zemin in 1997 while doing laps in the pool at Hickam AFB. We had talked, but I hadn't found out until later that he was the president of China. I asked Xi if he would ban all sales of wild animals at wet markets in his country. About two weeks later, I heard that he had done just that and Donald Trump didn't know why. But now, unfortunately, Indonesia started selling these animals.

On March 19, Mayor Kirk Caldwell shut down all city parks and golf courses. It was like closing the henhouse after all the chickens had gotten out. I still swam because they couldn't shut down the ocean. At least I get my daily exercise, while the rest of Hawaii was hunkered down and only allowed out to buy food or go to work or the hospital. Shops were starting to close, and people who worked and lived paycheck to paycheck were filing for unemployment. Store owners couldn't pay their rents or mortgages and were asking the government for help because they didn't have any money saved up. On March 24, Hawaii had its first death because of Governor Ige, the Department of Health's Dr. Anderson, and Mayor Caldwell. So, I wrote a letter to those three stooges and threatened to charge them with a criminal offense like California did to Governor Jerry Brown before he resigned after the fires killed thousands a couple of years ago.

The local blood bank was running low. So, I donated plasma for the first time since I'd left Tripler Medical Center two years ago, and they were a lot more professional. I met Elizabeth Lau in my building. She'd fractured her ankle and asked me to help her with the post office and grocery shopping. but she was getting a little bossy like Lisa had a few years ago. Then I found out she wasn't Chinese. I'd thought she was because she'd kept her ex-husband's last name. But, rather, she was also Korean. So, I'd already learned my lesson.

On April 9, cases worldwide were at 1.9 million, with 120,000 deaths. US cases were at 600,000, with 24,000 deaths. And Hawaiian cases were at 515, with 9 deaths. The stock market hit a low of 21,000, and I'd lost $10,000 at Edward Jones. But my gold was worth $1,780 an ounce. The virus curve was starting to flatten out, and we were working on a couple of vaccines, like hydroxychloroquine and Remdesivir. So maybe the worst was over—as long as we kept our distance from one another and wore face masks, the United States would rebound. God had caused this pandemic because the world was getting overcrowded and we were destroying our environment.

But a bit of good news—the skies over large cities around the world were clear for the first time in decades, children in Beijing could finally see the buildings, sun, and stars.

On May 3, it was my seventy-ninth birthday, and countries all around the world were in lockdown, making people stay at home except for emergencies. The global virus count was at 3.6 million, with 252,000 deaths. US cases had hit 1 million, with 68,000 deaths. Hawaii had 625 cases, with 17 deaths, with the curve still getting better. Three times a week, four thousand cars around Oahu lined up at food distribution centers because people had nothing to eat but were driving $50,000 pickups. I was sure that, if and when this pandemic was under control, people would start living within their means and quit wasting our resources. But if we had a second wave this fall and Africa and India got hit, they could lose as many as 200 million people, mainly from starvation.

It wasn't all bad news. On May 30, Elon Musk launched his SpaceX rocket, partnered with NASA and with two astronauts to the International Space Station. It was the first time in ten years. We no longer had to depend on Russia, saving us a ton of money. The rocket boosters were recovered to be used again, costing a tenth what the government space shuttle used to cost.

On Memorial Day 2020, the United States started to relax the lockdown, with people going to the beach in large groups and having barbecues and shopping and some without wearing masks. I was afraid there would be a spike in the virus. In fact, on June 21, the world cases passed 9 million, with 450,000 deaths; the US cases were at 2 million, with 120,000 deaths; and Hawaii had 800 cases with 17 deaths. The Democrats have failed to impeach Donald Trump, so now they were destroying our cities by paying professional black rioters and looters to burn buildings and take down statues all over the country, agitating the younger generation and dividing blacks and whites from one another more than ever.

I finally received the payoff on my Silver Springs property and made another $5,000 in interest over the past year. So, I paid off my condo in Hawaii with navy federal—what a relief.

Joe Biden and Kamala Harris announced their nomination for the DNC president and vice president of the United States, but they were both liars and crooks. The Hawaii House politicians finally fired Department of Health Director Dr. Bruce Anderson and Public Safety Department Director Nolan Espinda for dereliction of duty regarding COVID-19; the governor and mayor would be next.

It was September 1, 2020, and the virus cases and death totals were up—worldwide, 26 million / 860,000; in the United States, 6 million / 188,000; and in Hawaii 8,500 / 70 respectively. The blood bank was taking two units of platelets from me every two weeks, causing me to faint. The good news was my O positive blood type was less likely to clot if I contacted the virus.

The aluminum handle on my golf cart finally broke after ten years. So, I made a new one instead of buying a new card; I saved $200, and it was stronger than before. I thought my car was running rich but found out later that someone was siphoning gas out of the tank in the parking garage due to poor security. So, I finally moved my car to another garage after fifteen years, with better security and cheaper rates.

Biden finally won the forty-sixth presidency by stealing votes but nobody got caught. What a bunch of assholes. Israel assassinated a top nuclear scientist in Iran, trying to stop their production.

It was 2021, and Pfizer had developed a vaccine that required two shots within a month. But the United States was having trouble with priorities in terms of who got the shots first.

My left sinus cavity had been getting more and more blocked for years. So, I went to an ENT who removed twelve polyps; it was the first time since 1980. I guess it was hereditary because my father had them.

The virus count for cases and death was now world 105 million / 2 million; US 27 million / 435,000; and Hawaii 26,000 / 416. But it should finally start leveling off.

Democratic protesters stormed the US Capitol, leaving four dead, and blamed it on Donald Trump. This feud between the parties would never stop. Trump finally left the White House and moved to his retreat at Mar-a-Lago in Florida to play golf and plot his return in 2024. Pfizer got its vaccine approved, and thanks to Trump's Operation Warp Speed, the world was getting vaccinated. We had a lightning storm in Oahu in March, flooding the North Shore, and our governor wouldn't do anything; he had to go.

All my lights in the Ranchero went out one morning going up the Pali Highway. Malcomb at Punahou Auto sold his business, and the new owner was a businessman, not a mechanic. His young crew spent a week changing parts but couldn't find the problem. So, I found Collin at Makiki Auto, who replaced the alternator in two hours. He also located an emergency brake release system from a Lincoln Continental on the mainland, so it seemed I'd found a new mechanic.

I received the first vaccine shot on my birthday and the second shot three weeks later. But I didn't trust the medicine and still wore a mask and practiced social distancing.

The Honolulu Area Rapid Transit (HART) was still running into problems, and the cost had skyrocketed to $12 billion and may never get finished. There was a new Delta variant virus that came from India and was spreading all over the United States, including Hawaii. And some people refused to get vaccinated. The Tokyo Olympics was held this summer with no spectators. And the world virus count was at 220 million / 5 million; US 40 million / 660,000; and Hawaii 650,000 / 675.

That stupid Kamala Harris was sent down to our southern border to stop the illegal human traffic. But she overflew Mexico and landed in El Salvador to visit her relatives and then came back to Washington without doing her job. What a useless VP. The first thing sleepy Joe Biden did when he took office was to sign bills that reversed everything Donald Trump had accomplished, including stopping construction on the wall. The illegal aliens knew it and started coming by the thousands.

On November 24, I received a booster shot from Pfizer and should be good for about a year. But another variant emerged from Africa called Omicron and was killing Africans by the thousands every day. Pfizer said the booster should help, but their scientists were working on another vaccine.

I started playing tennis after a year, with the time away due to the virus. But my knees started hurting again. I went to the VA and had both knees shot with Gel-One. Why did I wait so long?

I finally had new rotors installed on the front brakes, a repair needed thanks to the steep Pali Highway. It cost $700.

The navy had an underground fuel storage at Red Hill near Pearl Harbor that was installed during World War II. But in 2014, there was a small leak the navy didn't disclose to the public. The fuel tanks were above a freshwater aquifer that supplied water to about 100,000 residents. In May 2021, another leak was discovered, and on December 2, a fuel smell was detected in tap water at homes near the storage facility. The navy denied any leaks at first but changed its minds when people got sick and had to move out of their homes. President Biden finally declared a national emergency in Hawaii and told the navy to shut down the system. But it would take a while.

I wrote Senators Hirono and Schatz and the regional commander, Admiral Kott, but had not received any response as of this writing. Our senators spend most of their time in Washington, DC, and don't realize how precious our water system is here on the island.

SUMMARY

I've had a challenging life. At times I didn't think I would live this long. But sometimes God does things in mysterious ways. The world has changed considerably, and I was fortunate to be brought into a loving family that stood behind me and taught me right from wrong and how to give more than to take; it's a better feeling. I wasn't the smartest kid in school, but my mother showed me how to work and get what you want and try to learn from your mistakes. I made a lot of friends and some enemies but always tried to maintain a sense of humor and enjoyed making people laugh, regardless of how bad the situation was.

If I had to do it over again, I wouldn't change anything except that you should look before you leap and shouldn't take things for granted. When I was younger, money was very important, but as I aged, knowledge and health were more satisfying. The '50s and '60s were an innocent time. Then came the Vietnam War, and people became reckless with sex, drugs, and demonstrations, saying it was not their war, and the government was lying to them. Then came the '70s and '80s. We were sending astronauts to the moon on a space shuttle, people were spending money because of low interest rates, and the economy was very strong, with everyone driving big gas-guzzling cars creating smog in large cities. Then the AIDS virus arrived with no cure. The '90s were the beginning of computers, and the elite were walking around with large cell phones that weighed a pound or two. In 2000, Tiger Woods was a golf sensation, and we started fighting other country's wars in Somalia, Libya, Iraq, and Afghanistan. No wonder we had so many enemies.

Computers have now taken over our lives, with countries hacking one another all over the world. The older generation are unable to keep up with the new technology, and I consider myself an old dinosaur and have trouble operating a smartphone or logging onto the internet. In fact, when I arrived in Hawaii twenty years ago, I went into Comp USA and asked the young salesperson where the typewriters were, and he wouldn't stop laughing.

Families are changing, with same-sex marriages, and while parents are both working, the children have no guidance, with drug use common and suicide rates high. Young people don't respect their elders, and crime and murders are taking place all over our country. Maybe if and when this pandemic is ever under control, this world will return to the basics, but I don't know.

Printed in the United States
by Baker & Taylor Publisher Services